THE BATTLE OF MINE CREEK

THE BATTLE OF MINE CREEK

The Crushing End of the Missouri Campaign

JEFFREY D. STALNAKER
SERIES EDITOR DOUG BOSTICK

THE History PRESS

Published by The History Press
Charleston, SC 29403
www.historypress.net

Cover image: *Charge at Mine Creek*, by Andy Thomas.

First published 2011

Manufactured in the United States

ISBN 978.1.60949.332.5

Stalnaker, Jeffrey D.
The Battle of Mine Creek : the crushing end of the Missouri campaign / Jeffrey D. Stalnaker.
p. cm.
Includes bibliographical references and index.
ISBN 978-1-60949-332-5
1. Mine Creek, Battle of, Kan., 1864. 2. Price's Missouri Expedition, 1864- 3. Kansas--History--Civil War, 1861-1865. I. Title.
E477.16.S73 2011
978.1'031--dc23
2011036868

This book is dedicated to my two beautiful girls: my wife, Jen, and my daughter, Emma. With their encouragement and support I have been able to fulfill my lifelong dream of becoming a writer.

Contents

Acknowledgements

There are so many people, elements, sources and historical figures I would like to thank for this book. The first person I would like to thank with all of my being is my unbelievable editor, Douglas Bostick. He is an accomplished author who took the time to consider a new author to relate the story of the Battle of Mine Creek. Without his patience, knowledge, guidance and good nature, I simply could not have done this. He is a man to whom a thousand thanks are due, and I will be forever in his debt.

U.S. Army senior historian Kendall Gott, at Fort Leavenworth, is another who can never be repaid. He took time out, more than once, to sit and allow me to fire questions his way. His deep understanding of Price's raid is remarkable. To listen to a real military mind talk about the battles, mindsets and aims gives a special perspective to the Missouri Campaign as a whole and actually helped to place me in the saddle with the Union and Confederate troopers.

I also want to acknowledge the late Lumir Buresh. His book *October 25th and the Battle of Mine Creek* is the standard by which the Battle of Mine Creek is studied. It was a very technical and well-researched book that gives a true framework for the battle and the way it unfolded. His gift to the world of U.S. Civil War scholarship is one that still stands the test of time.

The help I received from the research libraries is also much appreciated. I especially want to thank the University of Kansas Watson Library and the Spencer Research Library. My alma mater proved, once again, to have an immense amount of valuable resources for me. Many people at all of the particular research institutions were willing to step in and lend a hand with any question I had.

I also spent some great time on the telephone with Arnold Schofield, administrator of the Mine Creek Battlefield State Historic Site. He was willing to field several calls from me and runs a great historic site that is a treasure for the state of Kansas. This hallowed ground is located just south of Pleasanton, Kansas, at 20485 Kansas Highway 52. It is well worth a visit to walk the battlefield and soak up the history in person.

I need to acknowledge Andy Thomas for allowing me to use his wonderful work, *The Charge at Mine Creek*, for the cover of this book. It is a truly masterful work and helps to set a wonderful tone for it even before you open it.

There are many other people who, even in the smallest of ways, helped me with this book. To them, I say thank you. This work is the fulfillment of a lifelong dream.

Most of all, however, I have to thank my family and friends for their incredible support. My wife, Jen, my daughter, Emma, and the rest of my amazing family stood beside me and allowed me to spend countless hours in my office trying to find the words to convey the story of the Battle of Mine Creek in some competent manner.

Lastly, to the Union and Confederate troopers who faced the bullets and laid down their lives for the cause they believed in, I owe a priceless debt. Many were left on the battlefield. Let none of us ever forget the sacrifice that you made in the name of freedom.

Introduction

History is most often written by the victors and not the vanquished. The Battle of Mine Creek is no exception. On October 25, 1864, on the gently rolling plains of eastern Kansas, Union forces under the joint commands of Major Generals Samuel Curtis and Alfred Pleasonton caught up with the rear guard of Major General Sterling Price's twelve-thousand-strong army after a two-day rapid pursuit following the massive Union victory at the Battle of Westport in Kansas City. After the first contact at the tiny hamlet of Trading Post, the Confederate troops under direct command of Major Generals John S. Marmaduke and James F. Fagan struggled to maintain a rear guard action that would prevent Curtis and Pleasonton's cavalry from reaching and destroying General Price's massive wagon train laden with supplies, prisoners, captured loot, weapons and food.

The climactic battle of the day occurred at Mine Creek, a small tributary to the Little Osage River near modern-day Pleasanton, Kansas. About 2,600 blue-coated cavalry troops, led by Colonel John F. Phillips and Lieutenant Colonel Frederick W. Benteen, stared down the guns of about 8,000 Confederate cavalrymen arrayed in a skirmish line that stretched nearly half a mile across. In a short but fierce battle, these Union troops completely smashed the Confederate forces and sent them scrambling farther south.

In his book *October 25th and the Battle of Mine Creek*, Lumir Buresh likens this charge to the charge of the British Light Brigade that had occurred exactly ten years before, on October 25, 1854, during the Battle of Balaclava in the

Crimean War. In terms of audacity in the face of seemingly insurmountable odds, this cannot be far from the truth. What a sight this must have been for these Union troopers.

This is the only battle of the entire American Civil War that took place in Kansas. It is largely ignored and nearly completely misunderstood. What makes this remarkable is the fact that it is among the largest cavalry battles of the entire war. When the opposing sides faced each other at Mine Creek, they numbered nearly eleven thousand in total. In terms of magnitude, the Battle of Mine Creek compares with many of the well-known battles in the East. Yet there was little newspaper coverage and few stories that related this mighty charge to the American public despite the fact that this battle effectively ended the Missouri Campaign in the Trans-Mississippi theater of operations. U.S. Army senior historian Kendall Gott said that "after this battle none of Sterling Price's forces get back into the war—Sterling Price's command is gone."

I hope to make this a book for all of the people of Kansas and Missouri, Civil War historians and those who simply want to read about a battle that took place so long ago on the wind-swept plains of Kansas. Can this be considered a great battle? I hope to show that it can be. From the origins of "Bleeding Kansas," the goals of Sterling Price's Missouri Campaign, the Battle of Westport and the aftermath, I hope to effectively relate the impact that the Battle of Mine Creek had on Kansas, Missouri, the Trans-Mississippi theater, President Lincoln's reelection in 1864 and the American Civil War as a whole.

Chapter 1

Bleeding Kansas

On the lintels of Kansas
That blood shall not dry;
Henceforth the Bad Angel
Shall harmless go by;
Henceforth to the sunset,
Unchecked on her way,
Shall Liberty follow
The march of the day.
—John Greenleaf Whittier, 1858

On the spring morning of May 19, 1858, a band of about thirty armed proslavery border ruffians, led by Georgia native Charles Hamilton, crossed the border from Missouri into Kansas territory. Hamilton had come to the border area only a couple of years before intent on aiding the proslavery faction, which was mostly from the state of Missouri, in swaying Kansas to become a slave state. This was just one instance of a string of occurrences that erupted on the border between Kansas and Missouri. These small clashes often involved looting, the burning of homes and businesses, the killing of cattle, beatings and, occasionally, deaths.

On this May morning, the situation on the border took a horrible turn. Hamilton had allegedly warned sometime before this day that "we are coming up there to kill snakes, and will treat all we find there as snakes." In a small ravine on the gently rolling prairie of eastern Kansas, he pointedly fulfilled his promise. During that day's foray into the territory, Hamilton and his men had rounded up eleven free state men. These men were completely unarmed, and most of them actually knew Hamilton since he had been in the area for a couple of years. The free staters, rounded up only because they favored keeping Kansas free from slavery, were marched into a hilly, secluded area and told to form in a line. Hamilton and his band of ruffians formed in a line opposite them. He then ordered his men to open fire and reportedly fired the first shot himself. After the first volley, they dismounted and used pistols to finish the deed. Of the eleven men, five were murdered on the spot. The rest were wounded, except for one man who had been untouched and had feigned being hit to escape the onslaught. Hamilton's band then turned and quickly fled for the safety of Missouri. This event became known as the "Marais des Cygnes Massacre" and was just one in a string of instances that caused famed editor of the *New York Tribune*, Horace Greeley, to label this troubled territory "Bleeding Kansas."

Many have argued that Kansas is the "Cradle of the Civil War." In 1854, the Kansas-Nebraska Act allowed the newly created territories of Kansas and Nebraska to use "popular sovereignty" to decide whether each would allow slavery or abolish it on its home soil. This would effectively negate the Missouri Compromise of 1820, which delighted a great many in the proslavery faction. By allowing "squatter sovereignty" to decide whether a state or territory would welcome slavery or not, the area radically changed

The Marais des Cygnes Massacre. *Courtesy of the Kansas State Historical Society.*

U.S. senator Stephen A. Douglas.
Courtesy of the Library of Congress.

the way that the ever expanding country could take shape. Under the Missouri Compromise, "slavery was prohibited in the former Louisiana Territory north of the parallel 36°30' north except within the boundaries of the proposed state of Missouri." Within the framework of the Kansas-Nebraska Act, each of these new territories could enter the Union and be permitted to be slave-owning areas. The Kansas-Nebraska Act was penned by Senator Stephen A. Douglas, a prominent U.S. senator from Illinois. Senator Douglas hoped that this would effectively end years of often bitter debate between slaveholders and abolitionists by offering what he considered a "concession to the Southern states" allowing slavery in territories that were currently not open to slavery in the North and West.

Suddenly, Kansas mattered. With the passing of the Kansas-Nebraska Act, the newly formed Kansas and Nebraska Territories were effectively open to settlement by pioneers heading west in droves, seeking land and new lives. The result of this touched off a firestorm of political fighting and ignited a "proxy war" that reverberated throughout the United States and ultimately was a precursor to the American Civil War. The Kansas Territory and the western parts of Missouri became a microcosm of the slavery issue that had been raging for years. Among the settlers were proslavery sympathizers primarily from Missouri and other parts of the South and abolitionists primarily from the North, many from New England.

Missouri, a slave state, certainly had a vested interest in seeing Kansas join the ranks of slave states. It was currently bordered by Iowa and Illinois, both free states, and Arkansas, a slave state. If Kansas were to become a free state, it would mean that Missouri would now be surrounded by free state territory, with the exception of Arkansas. This was viewed by proslavery Missouri as a considerable threat. If it was to be surrounded on three sides by free states, then it could reasonably be expected that an even greater increase of abolitionist activity would occur, including escapes and Underground Railroad aid. The Kansas-Nebraska Act gave the slave state faction a new hope in keeping the "status quo" since up to this point there were about the same number of slave states as there were free states. Under the Missouri Compromise, any new states entering the Union would be free. Under the Kansas-Nebraska Act, the decision could go either way. The stage was set for battle.

Initially, most of the new settlers were proslavery due to the proximity to Missouri. They had a short distance to travel to set up communities in towns such as Atchison, named for ardent slavery supporter Senator David Rice Atchison, and Leavenworth. The result of this early flow of proslavery settlers was that, at the outset at least, Kansas appeared well on the way to becoming a slave state. Once the slave staters arrived in Kansas, they began to exert their influence on the political scene in the new territory. While the Free Soilers were later to arrive, they slowly set up initially around the "Free State Fortress" of Lawrence and were ready to use their influence to ensure that Kansas was free.

By the spring of 1855, it was time for territorial elections. Missourians were ready. Thousands were exhorted to form in large groups to travel to Kansas and vote. "General" James H. Stringfellow said that "[f]amilies with all their slaves are making preparations to move as soon as the weather will permit." He also called for his fellow slave staters to "vote at the point of the bowie-knife and the revolver." This type of furor was intense on both sides of the debate. Although there were only about two thousand registered voters in Kansas at the time of the territorial elections, there were about six thousand ballots cast due to this questionable tactic by the slave staters.

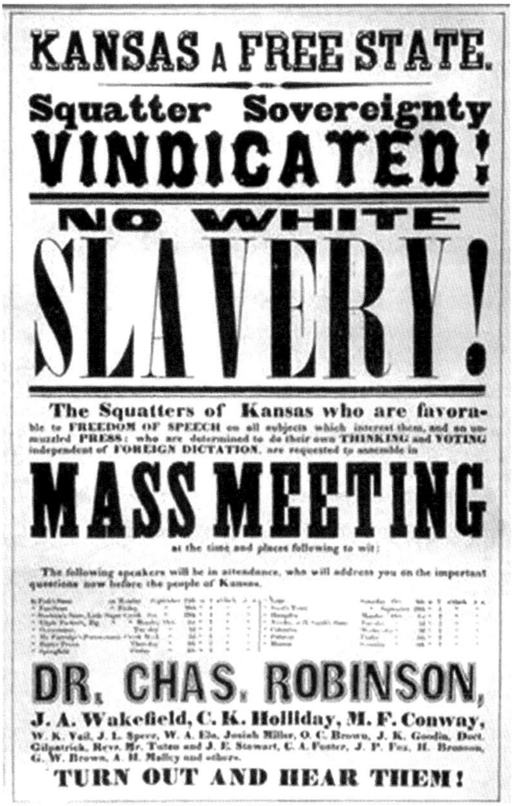

An antislavery ad. *Courtesy of the Kansas State Historical Society.*

A "Bleeding Kansas" poster. *Courtesy of the Kansas State Historical Society.*

Southern chivalry: argument versus club. *Courtesy of John Magee.*

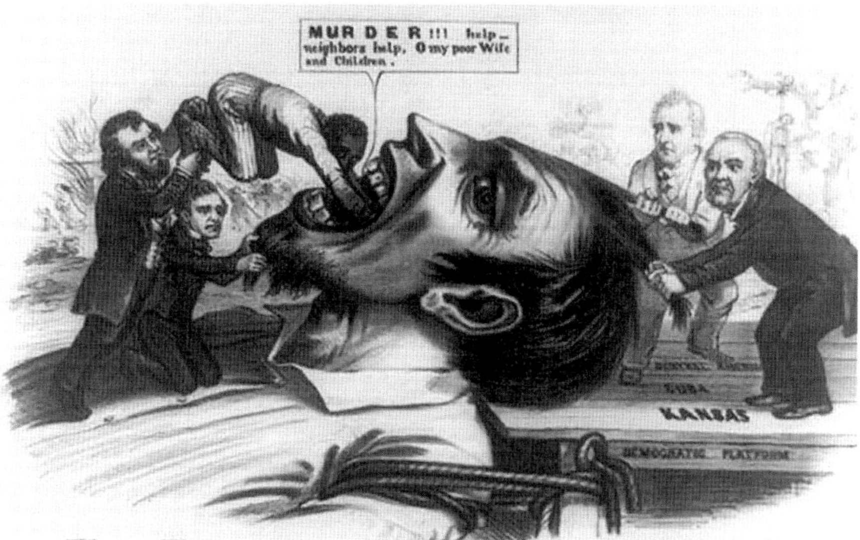

"Forcing Slavery Down the Throat of a Freesoiler." *Courtesy of John Magee.*

Kansas governor Andrew H. Reeder was in a quandary after this election. He was tormented about the decision but knew that President Franklin Pierce's administration would "roar if he made trouble."

The question now was whether to declare the election a fraud and call for a new one. Governor Reeder "had been threatened bodily and might be killed" if he were to completely overturn the election, so he decided to call it valid but threw out many ballots and called for new elections to be held in many of these districts. This, for obvious reasons, did not sit well with the free staters.

The free staters now began arriving in greater numbers, intent on Kansas being a Free Soil state. A great number from this influx came from New England and were aided, and often armed, by the New England Emigrant Aid Company. Founded by New Englander and future Massachusetts congressman Eli Thayer, its purpose was to facilitate the transport of people from the East to Kansas to swing the electorate in the favor of those opposing slavery. One notable northeasterner was a man named Henry Ward Beecher. Beecher was a preacher and an ardent abolitionist. He preached feverishly against slavery and began to collect money for the settlers. His main contribution was to fund the purchase of relatively new and highly sought Sharps rifles. These rifles were to become known as "Beecher's Bibles." These new Kansas abolitionists were now armed and ready to take the fight to their new enemies, the border ruffians.

Eli Thayer. *Courtesy of the Spencer Museum Collection, the University of Kansas.*

New England Emigrant Aid Company. *Courtesy of the Kansas State Historical Society.*

Among the towns founded by these free staters were Topeka and, most notably, Lawrence, which quickly earned the reputation of being a "Free State Fortress." Some of the early skirmishes between the opposing ideological forces occurred in and around Lawrence. From November to December 1855, the "Wakarusa War" began and was centered on the river valley of the Wakarusa, which is located very near to Lawrence. Although this "war" saw little bloodshed—only one man was killed—it was indicative of the type of skirmishes on the border between Kansas and Missouri. The man killed, incidentally, was named Thomas Barber. He would be considered somewhat a martyr for the free staters and was immortalized in a poem by John Greenleaf Whittier entitled "The Burial of Barber":

Bear him, comrades, to his grave;
Never over one more brave
Shall the prairie grasses weep,
In the ages yet to come,
When the millions in our room,
What we sow in tears, shall reap.
Bear him up the icy hill,
With the Kansas, frozen still
As his noble heart, below,
And the land he came to till
With a freeman's thews and will,

And his poor hut roofed with snow.
One more look of that dead face,
Of his murder's ghastly trace!
One more kiss, O widowed one
Lay your left hands on his brow,
Lift your right hands up, and vow
That his work shall yet be done.
Patience, friends! The eye of God
Every path by Murder trod
Watches, lidless, day and night;
And the dead man in his shroud,
And his widow weeping loud,
And our hearts, are in His sight.
Every deadly threat that swells
With the roar of gambling hells,
Every brutal jest and jeer,
Every wicked thought and plan
Of the cruel heart of man,
Though but whispered, He can hear!
We in suffering, they in crime,
Wait the just award of time,
Wait the vengeance that is due;
Not in vain a heart shall break,
Not a tear for Freedom's sake
Fall unheeded: God is true.
While the flag with stars bedecked
Threatens where it should protect,
And the Law shakes Hands with Crime,
What is left us but to wait,
Match our patience to our fate,
And abide the better time?
Patience, friends! The human heart
Everywhere shall take our part,
Everywhere for us shall pray;
On our side are nature's laws,
And God's life is in the cause
That we suffer for to-day.
Well to suffer is divine;
Pass the watchword down the line,

Pass the countersign: "Endure."
Not to him who rashly dares,
But to him who nobly bears,
Is the victor's garland sure.
Frozen earth to frozen breast,
Lay our slain one down to rest;
Lay him down in hope and faith,
And above the broken sod,
Once again, to Freedom's God,
Pledge ourselves for life or death,
That the State whose walls we lay,
In our blood and tears, to-day,
Shall be free from bonds of shame,
And our goodly land untrod
By the feet of Slavery, shod
With cursing as with flame!
Plant the Buckeye on his grave,
For the hunter of the slave
In its shadow cannot rest; I
And let martyr mound and tree
Be our pledge and guaranty
Of the freedom of the West!

In late 1855, one of the most powerful voices for abolition came to Kansas to fight for free state rights: John Brown. He said of slavery:

> *Whereas, Slavery, throughout its entire existence in the United States is none other than a most barbarous, unprovoked, and unjustifiable War of one portion of its citizens upon another portion; the only conditions of which are perpetual imprisonment, and hopeless servitude or absolute extermination; in utter disregard and violation of those eternal and self-evident truths set forth in our Declaration of Independence.*

John Brown was a true "revolutionary abolitionist" who believed that taking up arms against proslavery believers was the ultimate means to end slavery altogether.

On May 21, 1856, a group of border ruffians entered Lawrence and began ransacking the newspaper offices and looting in many other parts of the town. They also set fire to the Free State Hotel, as well as to several

John Brown. *Courtesy of the Kansas State Historical Society.*

homes. Many of Lawrence's residents had fled the town, so only one accidental death—ironically, a proslavery man—was reported. John Brown was particularly angered by this injustice done to his free state brethren and was ready to exact revenge. A few days later, on May 24, he got it in spades when, on three separate occasions, Brown and his group of men, including four of his sons, went to an area near Ottawa, Kansas, grabbed five men and hacked them to death with broadswords. This was another indication that both sides of the slavery debate were far from settled and that more blood would be shed along the border.

By 1856, the capital of the Kansas territory was moved to Lecompton, Kansas, a town situated a few miles west of Lawrence. The elections were fraudulent, as the free staters had argued. In April, President Pierce allowed a Congressional committee to investigate. The congressmen made their way to Kansas and, after sifting through the facts, declared in their statement "the elections to be improperly influenced by the border

Quantrill's Lawrence, Kansas raid. *Courtesy of the Kansas State Historical Society.*

The ruins of Lawrence, Kansas. *Courtesy of the Kansas State Historical Society.*

ruffians." President Pierce, clearly pro-Southern, took no action on these findings and continued to recognize what was considered by many to be a completely phony Kansas legislature as the legitimate government for the territory. In August of that year, an army of two to three hundred proslavery men led by John Reid and Reverend Marvin White crossed the border near Osawatomie intent on burning and looting the town and then moving on to Lawrence and Topeka. John Brown rounded up as many men as he could so that he could move to defend the town. He was able to put together an army that only numbered about forty men and tried desperately to halt the raid. In a battle that saw heavy fighting and a number of casualties, Brown's forces were swept away and Osawatomie was pillaged. The fighting continued for several more months.

By early 1857, the fighting had abated somewhat, due in large part to the efforts of new Kansas governor John Geary, appointed by President Pierce in September 1856. Geary aimed to appeal to both sides of the slavery debate for peace in Kansas: "I desire to know no party, no section, no North, no South, no East, no West; nothing but Kansas and my country." Still, the debate raged on, with intermittent skirmishes and continuous anger on both

A guerilla raid. *Courtesy of the Kansas State Historical Society.*

The Kansas legislative assembly. *Courtesy of the Spencer Museum Collection, the University of Kansas.*

sides of the debate. This turmoil became a microcosm of the American Civil War in the sense that the battle boiled down to pro-Southern rights for keeping this way of life on one side and the abolitionist values of freedom for "all mankind" on the other.

The fight in Kansas saw four different constitutions drawn up in Kansas: the Topeka Constitution (1855), the Lecompton Constitution (1857), the Leavenworth Constitution (1858) and the Wyandotte Constitution (1859). The first three of these works were not fitting to the majority of the Kansas Territory because of the interference of the proslavery supporters from Missouri territory. They were all, with the exception of the Wyandotte Constitution of 1859, largely boycotted by the free staters due to the unfairness of allowing the slavery factions to vote in them—therefore they didn't actually speak for the overall will of the people. In July 1859, state representatives met to draft a new covenant at Wyandotte, which is now a part of the Kansas City metro area. After completion, it was set for a referendum vote.

On October 4, 1859, it was voted on and approved by a two-to-one margin. The terms of this new constitution "rejected slavery," as spelled out in Section 6, which states: "There shall be no slavery in this State, and no involuntary servitude, except for the punishment of crime, whereof the party shall have been duly convicted." After passage, it went to the United States Congress. The House of Representatives passed it easily, but then it went to the Senate, where it met with a great deal of stiff opposition. At this time, however, the secession battle was waging, and as states began to leave the Union, their senators began to return home, which left an antislavery majority in the upper chamber. Without many of the Southern senators in attendance, the bill was put before the main body and was passed on January 21, 1861. Eight days later, on October 29, 1861, Kansas was admitted as the thirty-fourth state of the United States and was free of slavery.

Obviously, this was a huge victory for abolitionists throughout America and a great blow to the slaveholding states. The admission of Kansas as a free state was one of the final straws that led to the secession of the Southern states and, ultimately, to the American Civil War.

Chapter 2

The Missouri Campaign

The American Civil War had been dragging on for years, and the South was looking at the possible end of an era. The Confederate forces and their leadership were beginning to find it difficult to see how they could ultimately win a protracted war against the North—they simply couldn't match the Union's ability to field an army and properly supply it due to its superior manufacturing and transportation infrastructure. By mid- to late 1864, it was becoming increasingly clear that the Confederates needed a victory if they were to stay in the war and effect real change. The CSA was a year removed from the crushing defeat at Gettysburg, Atlanta was in the grasp of General Sherman and much of the rest of the South was controlled by Union forces that moved with impunity throughout the region. Additionally, President Lincoln was up for reelection, and Southern sympathizers and Confederates hoped that they could negatively affect his campaign and see him suffer defeat at the polls. If there was an opportunity to reverse their fortunes and turn the tide of the war, it would have to be in the Trans-Mississippi area, as this was the only place that seemed to offer any hope given the fact that, from a military standpoint, the war in the East was all but decided.

General Samuel Curtis, an ardent abolitionist, assumed command of the Department of Kansas and Indian Territory, which had been a fairly quiet area throughout the early part of 1864. Rebel troops had been fairly inactive, with the exception of the bushwhackers who continued to harass free staters in northern Missouri. At this point, Union leadership felt that a defensive

Above: The Battle of Pea Ridge, Currier & Ives. *Author's collection.*

Left: Union general Samuel Curtis. *Courtesy of the Kansas State Historical Society.*

posture in the Trans-Mississippi would be much more beneficial for the war effort as an overall strategy and that the bulk of the forces should concentrate on the task at hand in the Southeast given the two-front viewpoint.

The situation south of Missouri and Kansas, under the leadership of General E. Kirby Smith, looked far better for the Rebels. The spring of 1864 saw several major Confederate victories in the Trans-Mississippi, including the Camden Expedition and in the Red River Campaign. This made the state of affairs in Arkansas very difficult for the Union troops under Major General Frederick Steele, commander of the Department of Arkansas. After holding control of the area for quite some time, they suddenly were forced to the northern part of the state and experienced a limited ability to counter Major General Sterling Price and his forces, which drove the Union forces back toward Little Rock and left them with little ability to move from these fortifications and push back at the Rebel army. The Confederates needed to make a move soon if they were to stem the tide of the war and capitalize on the recent successes in the Trans-Mississippi.

Missouri was, in late 1864, a prime target for the underutilized Rebel troops west of the Mississippi. It was decided that General Sterling Price would lead a Confederate army into Missouri. Sterling Price was a logical choice because he was a son of Missouri. He was a farmer and a lawyer and was also a former governor of the state who filled the office from 1853 to 1857. It was decided that he could lead an army into the state from northern Arkansas and capture it once and for all for the Confederacy. Missouri never seceded from the Union formally and had split loyalties among the citizenry about what side the state should stand on. It was a slave state, and many Missourians argued that they shared a much stronger bond with the South than with the North—even going so far as to earn the nickname "Little Dixie."

The Confederates hoped that intelligence reports coming from the area were true. The war had dragged on for many years and was a drain on manpower, property and money. It was thought that a Rebel army rolling through Missouri would be able to bring the state together and into the Confederacy. The exiled Confederate governor, Thomas C. Reynolds, was to accompany the march and be installed as official governor once the army was able to capture Jefferson City after also plundering St. Louis of military supplies and men. If the force could occupy the state long enough, and Governor Reynolds could muster the greater share of popular support, this could become reality. These same intelligence reports also suggested that groups in Missouri would gladly support an invasion of the state and wished to help ensure that the Union army would have to siphon troops from the important operations in the East to help repel operations in the Trans-Mississippi. This would draw valuable U.S. troops and matériel from the zones in the East and perhaps buy extra time for the Confederacy to ultimately expel the Yankees from the South. A successful Missouri campaign could also put a serious damper on President Abraham Lincoln's upcoming reelection campaign by garnering support of those in Lincoln's "War Party." If Missouri were to leave the Union and Lincoln was to be subsequently defeated in 1864, the Confederacy would then be in a far better situation to end the war as a separate nation.

Militarily, this was to be executed boldly, utilizing about twelve thousand cavalry and mounted infantry troops marching out of Arkansas and led by Major General Price. Two other Missourians would also be in the vanguard of the Confederate army: General John S. Marmaduke and General Jo O. Shelby. Marmaduke was an educated man who had spent two years at Yale before transferring to Harvard and, ultimately, ending his education at the U.S. Military Academy at West Point. He was wounded at the Battle of Shiloh and was made a division commander before the Missouri Campaign. Jo Shelby came from a wealthy Missouri family and made quite an impact during the Civil War in Missouri. He formed a cavalry company early in the war and performed extremely well in the Trans-Mississippi.

Price's military goals for the Missouri Campaign were very ambitious and were designed to deliver Missouri from under Union control. The first objective was St. Louis, which was seen as a treasure-trove of military equipment, armaments and supplies. To capture this city would help to separate Missouri from the rest of the Union and give the Confederacy a base on the Mississippi River. The forces would then move westward toward Jefferson City, capture the city and install Governor Reynolds as the Confederate governor, effectively delivering the state to the Confederacy. They were then to move farther west toward Kansas City. Fort Leavenworth, Kansas, was also supposed to have a great store of military supplies and weapons, and Price wanted to capture them as well.

After a successful capture of Fort Leavenworth, Price was to turn south and journey through eastern Kansas capturing what he could and destroying all that stood in his way. After leaving Kansas, the army would be able to find safe haven in Arkansas or continue through Indian Territory and on to Texas. The invasion would also need to be a fairly self-sustaining expedition and would require a fairly slow pace because time would be needed to forage for supplies and recruit men to fill the ranks. Also known was the fact that Price was a former infantry commander, who normally travel at

Confederate general Sterling Price. *Courtesy of the Missouri State Historical Society.*

a much slower pace than cavalry or mounted infantry. This type of foray would most certainly need to be embraced by the people of Missouri. For this reason, it was extremely important to have a Missourian, Price, and two other Missourians, Marmaduke and Shelby, leading the raid.

On the morning of September 19, 1864, the Rebel army, called the Army of Missouri, advanced out of northern Arkansas and into Missouri. Among the Confederate units were two Missouri divisions led by Marmaduke and Shelby, as well as one division of troops from Arkansas commanded by Major General James F. Fagan, an Arkansas farmer and public servant. The forces numbered about twelve thousand men. Many of the men, near four thousand, were not armed and were expected to find something during the march through the state. The troops in the field carried a mixture of arms, with most of them armed with muzzleloading rifles in comparison to the Union cavalry troopers, who were generally armed with far superior breech-loading rifles or carbines. Union troopers were also often armed with multiple pistols and were issued a cavalry saber. This difference in firepower would play a critical part in the major battles of Price's raid as time wore on.

In addition to the differences in arms, Confederate troops also differed from their Union counterparts in uniform. The uniform for the Confederate troopers was a very simple one and was generally irregular. Oftentimes it was what the volunteer happened to already own. Gray was the most standard color, but others could be seen. They wore their own coats and were not of the same quality of the Union troops. Headwear was also a hodgepodge of styles, with many opting for their personal slouch hats. Many of the Rebel forces also wore Union blue uniforms since they simply had nothing military to wear. This would prove a costly and confusing quandary in the upcoming Battle of Mine Creek, causing much disorder when the forces were intermingled during and immediately following the battle. There were also many reported instances of Confederate troopers being shot for wearing the Union blue, given the bad blood between the opposing forces and the assumption that a Union soldier was killed, wounded or captured to get it.

On September 19, Price's columns started north out of Arkansas and headed into Missouri at a spot near Doniphan. The Missouri Expedition, as the Confederates called it, was moving toward the first objective at Pilot Knob. Union commanders had a great deal of intelligence that led them to believe that an invasion of Missouri was imminent. Major General William Rosecrans, head of the Union Department of Missouri, was almost certain of this and began the preparation of the state, strengthening it and buttressing the defenses in St. Louis by rerouting any available troops from places around Missouri, including one of A.J. Smith's divisions, which had been based at Cairo, Illinois, up to that point. He would certainly need this unit if Price hit St. Louis. He also placed the Missouri State Militia on alert and generally attempted to find any man he could put into the field to fight the invasion. The Missouri State Militia was a special force that was an unofficial part of the Union forces and received arms and uniforms, as well as payment. It mustered troops who operated within the border of the state of Missouri and was composed of cavalry for the most part. The militia's primary responsibility was the defense of Missouri, and members spent most of their time chasing bushwhackers. In addition to the Missouri State Militia, there was also a force called the Enrolled Missouri Militia. Both of these units would play a major part in the defense of Missouri during Price's raid and in the Battle of Mine Creek a few weeks hence.

The Confederates also launched, in conjunction with the Missouri Expedition, a diversion aimed at Fort Gibson, which stood on the Arkansas River. About two thousand men under the command of Brigadier General Richard Gano moved north out of Indian Territory across the Arkansas River and came upon a group of Union soldiers who were foraging for fodder for the horses at nearby Fort Gibson. General Gano's command, including artillery and Native American troops of General Stand Watie's Indian Brigade, quickly surrounded and subdued the Union soldiers, including a number of African Americans. All seventy-three of these African Americans were killed by Gano's troops. The band was also able to capture about eighty-five of the white soldiers. Gano then moved his force toward Fort Gibson and soon ran across a Union wagon train carrying supplies near Cabin Creek, which also featured a small fort. Major Henry Hopkins commanded this train, which included on it men from three Kansas regiments and also an Indian force that numbered about three hundred men. Altogether, Major Hopkins's strength was about one thousand men and included 250 wagons. On September 19, the same morning when Price's expedition moved into Missouri many miles away, Gano's forces attacked the Union wagon train. The Rebels quickly overran the Union force, destroyed many of the wagons and inflicted significant casualties, including "about 35" killed. The casualties were left on the battlefield due to Hopkins's quick action in banding together as many of the remaining forces as he could, despite being surrounded, pulling together about half of his remaining wagons, quickly moving out of the area and ultimately reaching Fort Gibson.

Meanwhile, Price's men had moved into Missouri on the same day. The expedition met some resistance along the way in the form of local militia units, but nothing that could stand in the way of his overwhelming force. In two days' march, Price had made it as far as Fredericktown, Missouri, and as was typical of his army, they picked the town through, grabbing food and supplies as they wished. As stated earlier, this was an army that was expected to forage for men, matériel and food throughout. It was difficult for some of the local citizens to come to grips with a "liberating force" looting and pillaging their precious food, water, cattle and private property.

General Rosecrans, still not positive as to Price's objectives, finally received definitive information about the location of Price's army on the twenty-fourth when he received intelligence that General Shelby's men had been spotted to the south of Pilot Knob. He immediately ordered Brigadier General Thomas Ewing—the man made famous (or infamous) for his Order 11, which forced settlers in four Missouri counties to leave the area completely unless they could prove their allegiance to the Union and was often enforced with great brutality—to move to Pilot Knob with as many men as he could muster. He was able to pull together several companies of the Fourteenth Iowa, numbering about two hundred, and left for Pilot Knob. When he got there, he was charged with figuring out the direction that Price and his column were moving and deciding whether the fort was in their path.

On the twenty-sixth, Ewing and his men reached Fort Davidson, which was located just outside of Pilot Knob. They then began scouting the area to see if they could discover the route that Price's army would take to reach St. Louis. The Rebels hoped to cut the railroad line that went to St. Louis, causing the Union forces to be completely cut off. Having done this, Price could have his way with the fort and its small detachment, which numbered just under one thousand men. Ewing, instead of taking his small command and moving it out of harm's way, decided to stand and fight Price, knowing all the while that, if captured, his fate would be sealed. He was severely hated by Price and his men because of Order 11 and would certainly be executed. Rosecrans specifically stated that General Ewing should take position on the area, but he was not to attack or even enter a firefight with Price's enormous force unless he thought that there was a reasonable chance of victory. If he could not go head to head and potentially emerge victorious, then he was to move to St. Louis, where the bulk of Rosecrans's forces were waiting. Ewing knew that he needed to do anything possible to delay Price's march and thereby allow additional time for St Louis to bring in troops for the defense of the city. "Let Missouri's Thermopylae be here!" it was declared.

Fort Davidson was a fine defensive position, consisting of

> *hexagonal walls nine feet high and ten feet thick, surrounded by a dry moat nine feet deep. Two long rifle pits ran out from the walls, while a reinforced board fence topped the earthworks. Access could only be had through a drawbridge on the structure's southeastern corner. A 300-yard cleared field of fire extended in every direction beyond the walls; any enemy approach would prove extremely hazardous.*

There were also a dozen artillery pieces mounted in gun positions, as well as rifle pits that were numerous throughout the exterior and could give cover to all of Fort Davidson's defenders. A magazine with four-foot-thick walls stood in the center of the fort.

On the twenty-sixth, Price's men ran into pickets set out some distance from the fort near the town of Ironton, which was just three miles from Fort Davidson. The pickets were there to fight a delaying action while falling back to St. Louis; this had been ordered by Rosecrans, but they were quickly overwhelmed and, despite spirited fighting through the streets of Ironton, were driven back to the fort. The next day, on the twenty-seventh, Price made the decision. He was not going to bypass the imposing fort, which prudence would have otherwise dictated. Instead, perhaps fueled by his hatred for Ewing, he made plans for battle. Two of his divisions, Marmaduke and his Missourians and Fagan and his Arkansas boys, would lead the attack. Marmaduke sent a rider under a flag of truce to Fort Gibson asking for Ewing's surrender. Ewing, aware of the Confederate predilection for killing prisoners in the Trans-Mississippi, said that he would fight. As Rebel forces moved closer and began to form for battle, another rider with a flag of truce approached the Union lines. Ewing, however, would not accept this flag. He made it known that if any other flags were to come forth, they would be met with gunfire. Shortly after that exchange, the Confederates began firing on the fort.

Fort Davidson sat between two sizeable mountains, Pilot Knob and Shepherd's Mountain. Price's forces were made to attack from four different directions. A number of the men were to move over the top of Pilot Knob, while another advance was made from the top of Shepherd's Mountain. A third force was to advance through the valley between the mountains, and a fourth was to advance around Shepherd's Mountain and hit the fort from the northeast. Rebels were able to secure several areas outside the fort and lay down cannon fire from a few of Marmaduke's guns. This fire did overwhelm a section of the gun pits and forced its evacuation. Fighting became fierce. Large Union guns rained canister fire onto the advancing Rebel forces. Ewing's men waited in their trenches until they were certain that Price's forward elements were in range of their rifles before they opened up. It was described that the men of the primary rank were cut down "like wheat straw before a scythe." Follow-up ranks also faced the horrendous fire from Union cannon and rifles yet still continued their advance, "shouting vengeance and death for the author of Order Number Eleven."

Coordination between the forces was extremely poor, with charges being made piecemeal instead of going in at the same time. This allowed the Union artillery batteries to consolidate fire on specific sections of the battlefield, beating off each successive charge. Brigadier General William L. Cabell's brigade, part of Fagan's division, was finally able to reach the moat in front of Fort Davidson despite the withering fire coming from the small detachment inside. When the brigade reached the nine-feet-deep moat, the troopers realized that there was no way to scale the walls and get at the defenders. They were forced to withdraw to their lines to fashion ladders for a second attack the next day. Night began to fall across the battlefield. Between six hundred and one thousand dead and wounded Rebels lay sprawled everywhere and littered the ground in front of the seemingly impregnable fort. Ewing's men fared far better, suffering only between one and two hundred casualties. General Price paid dearly for this assault but was still determined to take Fort Davidson.

General Ewing, having suffered few casualties, still realized that 25 percent of his command was out of action. He discussed his plan of action that night with the officers in his command. They decided that they could make a break for it and escape Fort Davidson and near certain annihilation. The brave defenders fashioned a bridge over the moat, and that they covered with a heavy canvass material that was designed to keep the sounds of the troopers' boots quiet and also muffle the noise that would certainly arise from the artillery wagons and horses' hooves as they crossed. They then planted a long fuse within the magazine and quietly marched off into the night. When they got safely out of range of Rebel ears, the rear guard lit the fuse and the powder magazine erupted.

The next morning, Price found the fort abandoned and the magazine in ashes. "Old Pap," a common nickname for Price, rashly sent Marmaduke and Shelby on a fruitless chase of Ewing's small detachment. After three days, they gave up and headed toward St Louis with Price's huge wagon train in tow. At Pilot Knob, Ewing did the best that could be expected given the vast difference in manpower. He and his men seriously affected Price's ability to push through Missouri at his own will and proved that the Union troops could stand toe to toe with them. This defeat also halted Price's advance for several days, just as General Ewing had predicted, and greatly aided the preparations for the defense of St. Louis.

Price's column snaked its way to St. Louis, facing men—many of them volunteers and local militia—in small units along the way, fighting a number of small engagements in which troopers took many prisoners and killed many defenders. As they had to at that point, and as they would throughout the campaign, they were able to loot the local area for supplies and armaments. A few days after the embarrassment at Pilot Knob, on September 30, General Price and his slow-moving, ever-growing column reached the St. Louis area and were able to get within approximately 30 miles of the city. There they found that the defenders were ready and waiting, including A.J. Smith's Corps of infantry, which numbered some four thousand troops. Having taken his lumps at Pilot Knob, Price decided that his best option was to abandon his plan to take the city and move west toward Jefferson City to his next objective: the capture of the capitol of Missouri and the installment of Governor Reynolds in the governor's office. The fact that the Army of Missouri had been delayed at Pilot Knob and had suffered a serious bloody nose was difficult enough for Price to swallow. He now had to abandon his first campaign objective, capturing St. Louis, and move on west. Had he bypassed Pilot Knob, fought off the small force from the rear and moved toward St. Louis quicker, he would have had additional manpower and more ammunition and the defenders would have had less time to prepare for their arrival. This series of events compounded to start the Missouri Campaign off to an inauspicious start.

The Rebel column was on the way west. There were objectives to meet, and this expedition still had a great chance of succeeding if they could keep on schedule. At his front, "General Ewing fought delaying skirmishes with the advancing army and read, in dispatches, that General Alfred Pleasonton was coming from St. Louis to strike Price in the rear," and "Pleasonton was a dangerous man to have at Old Pap's rear." During their journey, the Confederates were able to afflict a great amount of damage on the areas surrounding their march. They destroyed homes, bridges, railroad depots and any other structure that they felt was of importance. The column was continuing its plodding pace toward Jefferson City when Brigadier General John B. Sanborn received word that Price had abandoned his plans to take St. Louis and was headed toward Jefferson City. Sanborn was given orders to move his two brigades to Jefferson City and help fortify the city against attack. This needed to be done in great haste, as he was in a race with Price. He was able, due again to Price's deliberate movements and massive wagon train of supplies, to beat the Rebel forces there. General Sanborn and his men were able to make it to the crossing of the Osage River (just before Price and his column), get his army inside the city and add to the defenders already in place.

With the addition of Sanborn's brigades, total strength in Jefferson was raised to about six thousand troops and a significant amount of artillery. Lacking any siege cannons and still smarting from the defeat at Pilot Knob, Price stared up at the Missouri capitol on the hill that was now bristling with gun barrels and decided to forego an attack on Missouri's capital city. With that, the second important objective of his campaign was not to be realized. Reynolds, who was desperate to be installed in the capitol as the "rightful" governor of Missouri and deliver the state to the Confederacy, was furious. This rift between Price and Reynolds would continue to fester as the campaign wore on.

According to U.S. Army historian Kendall D. Gott, "Once the first two objectives fell apart, there is a paradigm shift in thinking. It changed from 'campaign' to 'raid.'" Gott went on to say that, at this juncture, Price "could have headed south out of Jefferson City with his forces intact, headed back to Arkansas, and waited for [General] Kirby Smith" to give them a mission. His command would still have been an effective fighting force at General Smith's disposal and could have made a difference in turning the tide in the Trans-Mississippi. Gott went on to say that Price "instead chose to raid." So, on October 7, they headed to Booneville. Booneville, Missouri, was one place that Price was certain that he would be welcomed as a conquering hero, as the area was "full of Confederate sympathizers." This made it a perfect place from which to launch his raid into the Kansas City area and then on into the heart of the state of Kansas.

The seventh also saw General Pleasonton arrive in Jefferson City soon after Price and his huge column had departed for Boonville. He was quick to take command of the troops in Jefferson City, forming them into a fighting unit that would dog Price throughout the rest of Missouri and into

An engraving of Jefferson City, Missouri. *Courtesy of the Missouri State Historical Society.*

Kansas City, then finally all the way to Mine Creek. Pleasonton, as has been described, "was a handsome middle-aged man with finely chiseled features," as well as a "confirmed bachelor" who "married the service." He had a great amount of experience in cavalry warfare, was a solid cavalry commander and had been involved already at two of the Civil War's large cavalry battles, Gettysburg and Brandy Station, where he performed quite well. He was the man responsible for helping to build up the Union cavalry forces and was now asked to take this knowledge and chase Price out of Missouri. He was now equipped, although severely outnumbered, to begin a rapid pursuit of Price. He had, as before, put General Sanborn's command in charge of the three brigades of cavalry in Jefferson City, and he would link up with Pleasonton to constantly hound Price's rear guard, which now was formed with two lead divisions in front of the advance and the third in the rear specifically tasked with keeping Pleasonton's men at bay.

Price's massive column rolled into Boonville on October 10, and as expected, they were treated as "Confederate liberators" as they "stacked arms, like Indian tepees, in the streets. Farmers and townsmen swarmed among the soldiers, inquiring for friends who had gone south." These men were, in large part, from Missouri, so they were home. "Brothers met and embraced, beard in beard." Supplies were plentiful in Boonville as men were able to find beds to sleep in and food to eat and generally enjoyed being in a town and out of the field, many for the first time in months. This was the first time since the Army of Missouri had crossed into the state that the men felt at home. Missouri was still a part of the Union, and the greater percentage of Missourians were pro-Union. Boonville, however, was a decidedly pro-Confederate city and was a much-needed breather for the Confederate forces. Price and his men spent a couple of precious days here gearing up for the upcoming opportunity to pounce on Kansas and exact revenge on the hated free state.

Chapter 3

Defeat at Westport

On October 14, Brigadier General John B. Clark, of Marmaduke's division, took two brigades and a few cannons across the Missouri River to attack the city of Glasgow. It was to be Price's only foray north of the river because of the fear that "Union steamboats could trap them north of the river," according to Gott. Glasgow was a small town but was armed and garrisoned with about nine hundred Federal soldiers. The attack was led by Clark, who was able to use his own brigade, which he placed under the command of Colonel Colton Greene, and added Colonel Jackman's brigade. The two brigades received covering fire from the opposite bank of the river that was supplied by a detachment of General Shelby's men, as well as by artillery that the force had brought with it. The attack was spirited and short. The Rebels lost a great number of men killed and wounded but eventually subdued the Federal detachment, and the town surrendered along with them. Along with the capture of Glasgow came the spoils, including rifles, coats, food and ammunition. They were able to arm a significant portion of the men in the army who had been previously unarmed. The overcoats also were of great benefit due to the changing late fall Missouri weather. These troops were beginning to struggle against the cold autumn nights.

The Army of Missouri was now committed to the raid into Kansas, and the Union commanders were coming to grips with this reality. The onus was now on them to figure out how they were going to stop Price and send him home defeated. All along the way toward Lexington, Missouri, Price's men cut telegraph wires and looted. Price, after having seen his first two objectives fail, according to Kendall Gott, needed something to "justify his existence so they had to keep going" so that they could take proof back to Rebel territory that the expedition was a success. This proof would be in the form of the huge wagon train of looted war matériel, personal possessions, cattle and prisoners. This wagon train made the entire column exceedingly slow—many of the wagons were pulled by oxen—as well as easy for the Union cavalry to track. Slowly but steadily, the Army of Missouri made its way toward Kansas City.

The defense of Kansas City and of the entirety of Kansas fell to Major General Samuel R. Curtis, who commanded the Department of Kansas. This department encompassed a huge area, including Nebraska, Colorado, Wyoming, portions of Utah and the Indian Territory. To do this, he had a force that totaled about four hundred troops. Curtis also had to maneuver through a maze of political gamesmanship with Kansas governor Thomas Carney to convince him to release the Kansas Militia to aid him in defense of the state. Carney was reluctant to do so because he became convinced that the request was simply a plot between General Curtis and Kansas senator James Lane to assure that the men who could vote in Kansas would be away from the polls. The election was within the next few months, and this, along with Lane's participation in a successful defense in Kansas, could dramatically aid his potential victory at the polls as well as the others in his faction.

Carney initially told Curtis that he would not call out the Kansas Militia unless he could be certain as to where Price was heading. Carney also went on to request that the "western counties share most of the burden of supplying the militia, since those on the border had been called upon many times before, those in the interior hardly at all." Ultimately, he had little choice but to call out the militia after receiving the definite word that he had requested. This came on October 9 from General Rosecrans and iterated that "Price had left Jefferson City and was moving westward in the direction of Leavenworth." Carney made the statewide call for "all men, white or black, between the ages of eighteen and sixty," to fall into the ranks of some type of military service. Along with this, Governor Carney instituted statewide martial law and proclaimed that the militia would remain "in the tented field until the rebel foe shall be beaten back."

Kansas became a tense state, with rumors running rampant that "Price was already above Kansas City. In Lawrence an accidental discharge of firearms created a near panic. At Leavenworth the sound of bells ringing and cannon firing to summon a citizens' defense rally caused 'wild anxiety' as the townspeople thought the rebels were upon them." All men who could shoulder arms took them and headed toward the "threatened border" ready to defend their homes and families. The extremely old and young, who were not called on to serve, were willing to play their part also by forming "home guard units." To the citizens of Kansas, this was total war, and they must be prepared. A.J. Ball, a young farm boy from near Mound City, was a part of Company K of the Eighteenth Kansas regiment. He was called out at Fort Scott because "old Rebel Price" was moving toward Kansas. Ball had been severely wounded in action at Jenkin's Ferry in Arkansas the previous April. He had only arrived in Fort Scott a few days before Price reached Kansas and was still on crutches. He was also still feeling the effects of his wounds. However, Ball, like many other Kansans young and old, was ready to do what he could to "help head off old Rebel Price's army," as Ball put it.

Ultimately, the Kansas Militia was organized into a unit and put under the command of General George Deitzler. He assembled his force of ten thousand militiamen near Kansas City on the Kansas side of the border, as Governor Carney had made it clear that the Kansas troops should not go into Missouri. This group of men was a ragtag group that was "poorly equipped and armed and badly deficient in training and discipline. Their only uniform consisted of a red badge pinned to their hats." General Curtis now had about fourteen thousand troops composing "the Army of the Border," which was divided into two divisions. General James Blunt, an ardent abolitionist and a man who had fought alongside Senator Lane, had been named to lead the District of Southern Kansas only days earlier. Blunt then formed three brigades and pegged three different men to lead them.

The first brigade was led by Colonel Charles R. "Doc" Jennison, who was one of the most feared of the Kansas Jayhawkers and led the Fifteenth Kansas Cavalry. The second brigade was formed under Colonel Thomas Moonlight, a Scottish-born leader of the Eleventh Kansas Cavalry throughout much of the war. The third of Blunt's regiments was led by Ohio-born Colonel Charles W. Blair, commander of the Fourteenth Kansas Cavalry and a man who fought throughout the Trans-Mississippi. Blunt's men took their positions as the right flank of the Army of the Border at Hickman Mills, Missouri. The left of the army was left to General Deitzler's division, which was the Kansas Militia. The fourteen-thousand-man army was now in position and awaited Price's certain advance into the Kansas City area. The defensive positions came after a compromise between General Curtis and Governor Carney, who finally succumbed to pressure to allow the Kansas Militia to cross the border into Missouri and move a short distance into the state. The army was

James Lane, U.S. senator from Kansas. *Courtesy of the Spencer Museum Collection, the University of Kansas.*

to make a stand at the Big Blue River, which ran just east of Kansas City and was about six miles across the Missouri state line. If the troops could not hold at the Big Blue, they were to fall back to an area just east of Kansas City. If that were an untenable position, then they would cross back into Kansas, take positions at the town of Wyandotte—which was just across the Kansas River—and make their stand there.

Several days passed without any word of Price's movements toward Kansas City. A great deal of infighting was taking place between the "Lane Faction" and those loyal to Governor Carney. Former governor Charles Robinson, a longtime Kansas abolitionist and supporter of Governor Carney, wrote that

> *it is beginning to be thought that our being called out is all a sham & a trick of Lane & Curtis's to make political capital. We cannot hear anything of importance as to the movements of Price. We think that we are being kept in*

> *ignorance of the true condition of affairs in order to keep the people out as long as possible. Steps are being taken to ascertain the facts. I have no doubt that Price has gone south & that there are only a few guerillas prowling about. Nobody thinks we shall have anything to do but go home in a few days & attend to our business.*

On the sixteenth, the situation began to intensify in Blunt's division as the politics worked to unravel the defending units. A regiment under Lieutenant Colonel James D. Snoddy, a Carney supporter, asked General Blunt if he could take his regiment and return south to Linn County. Blunt told him that he could not leave his position in the lines. Snoddy directly disobeyed Blunt, formed up his men and began to march toward home anyway. Upon hearing this news, Blunt took immediate action. He took with him two regiments, intent on stopping this desertion, and arrested the two commanders, Snoddy and Brigadier General William Fishback, for desertion and mutiny. This did not, however, stop a great number of militiamen from deserting anyway. Several days passed without any word of Price actually being in Missouri, and on the twentieth, Governor Carney requested that General Curtis end martial law so that he could release the militia members to return to their homes.

Price was continuing his advance toward Kansas City, and word would reach Curtis and Carney before the order could be given to release the militia. General Blunt took a detachment from his force, along with Senator Lane, and rode toward Pleasant Hill, Missouri, with about two thousand men. Leaving Pleasant Hill, they rode on to Lexington, where they ran into the forward elements of Price's column. This would begin the major piece of the fighting, which would move into the Kansas City area and begin the end of Price's Missouri Campaign. The Second Battle of Lexington, as it was called, was a minor engagement. The forward elements of Price's column clashed with Blunt's pickets and then ran into the main body of the force. A great deal of skirmishing took place, and Blunt initially was able to hold Price up, but after several rounds of fighting, Blunt knew that he had no chance to face Price's huge column with his meager force.

With that, the Second Battle of Lexington was over. This action was significant, however. Blunt was able to slow the Rebel advance yet again, as well as allow the Federal commanders a look at the size and disposition of the army that was bearing down on them. Blunt, under orders from Curtis, moved his force back toward Kansas City and took up positions on the Little Blue River between Lexington and along the route toward Independence. Curtis then ordered Blunt back to the lines in Independence. Before doing

An engraving of the First Battle of Lexington, Missouri. *Courtesy of the Missouri State Historical Society.*

this, he left six hundred of Colonel Moonlight's men behind to act as a delaying force in the hopes of halting Price's advance to buy more time for General Pleasanton's cavalry, who were still not in contact with the main body of Curtis's defense.

Price continued toward Independence on the twentieth without experiencing much in the way of resistance. On the twentieth, however, Marmaduke's division reached the Little Blue and began its attack. Colonel Moonlight's men were well entrenched behind rock walls and were quite unwilling to give up their ground to Price without a fight. The small force was no match for the numerical superiority that Marmaduke held, and Moonlight found himself being pushed back. An urgent request for reinforcements from Moonlight brought the two remaining brigades under Blunt's command into the action, and the Union forces were able to initially push back significantly, but Price called for Shelby to bring his forces to bear. Blunt's men, tired and running low on ammunition after the prolonged five-hour action, had to retire to a better position. Blunt withdrew back toward Independence and took up positions on the Big Blue River to the west, joining Curtis's troops and the Kansas Militia and hoping to give Pleasonton enough time to catch up with Price and begin an offensive against his rear.

The morning of October 22 dawned cool, and the respective forces prepared for the action of the day that was certain to come. By midday, the Rebels were set to attack. The Battle of Byram's Ford then ensued. Byram's Ford was the best river crossing point on the Blue River, and as stated previously, Price needed to find a good crossing over which to move his massive wagon train, which currently stood at about five hundred wagons. Price sent General Shelby to lead the charge, effect a crossing of the river at Byram's Ford and secure it for the rest of the army. At the same time, knowing that Curtis was still unsure where the Confederates would strike, Price sent a secondary decoy attack to the north end of the Union lines in the hopes of keeping troop movements to a minimum and aiding Shelby in his fight—and also with the hope that he could confuse General Curtis.

The Union troops had an excellent position on the west side of the bank, which was covered by areas where they had chopped down trees and placed other obstacles, and they were able to offer stiff resistance for quite some time. Eventually, Shelby took the initiative and ordered a flanking attack that finally saw the defenders in Blunt's division begin to peel away and move to their fallback position at Westport. By late afternoon, they had marched west and had reached Westport. According to reports, "Several regiments of raw militia tried to stem Shelby's advance on the prairies south of Westport, only to be ridden down and captured 'en masse.'" At this point, history has two different ways of analyzing the events. "According to Confederate sources Shelby could have kept going, but withdrew on his own accord with the approach of darkness. Federal accounts, on the other hand, state that Curtis' troops rallied and drove Shelby back, after which they voluntarily retired to Westport." What was clear, however, was that Blunt's cavalry in conjunction with the brave Kansas Militia were able to halt Price's advance just outside Westport. They had put up a magnificent fight and had lost a great many comrades. At this point, they were, after all, fighting to protect their home state from invasion.

General Pleasonton had still not been able to contact the rear elements of Price's vast army until late in the day on the twenty-second. After reaching Lexington on the morning of the twenty-first, Pleasonton was still unclear of the disposition of Curtis's troops and battle plans. Additionally, at this point, he had little reason to believe that the Kansas Militia could neither stand and fight nor be able to maneuver with his force in some semblance of order. Word finally got through to Pleasonton in the evening on the twenty-second. According to reports, "Daniel Boutwell, a volunteer scout from Curtis' army, contacted Pleasonton after a daring ride through guerilla-infested country and told him that Curtis was preparing to withstand Price on the Big Blue."

Pleasonton was ready to move now. He had the confirmation of Curtis's intentions and was ready to resume his drive to intercept Price. He reached Independence late in the afternoon on the twenty-second and encountered the rear guard of Price's force. He immediately hit the Confederate rear guard, which was a force that was part of Fagan's division and led by Colonel W.F. Slemmons; he then began pushing them steadily westward toward Independence. At this point, Price was between two forces. He had Curtis's main body to his west and Pleasonton's cavalry attacking him from the east. Finally, the rest of Fagan's division linked up with the beleaguered Slemmons. This wouldn't make a difference, however. The afternoon saw the Union forces making several charges against the Confederate lines in the city of Independence, where they took many prisoners and were able to capture several pieces of artillery.

The Rebels were being hit relentlessly and were being driven back to the Blue River. The brigade under Colonel Phillips began to bear down on Colton Greene's men and was hammering them relentlessly. It is reported that Greene's men were able to escape from Phillips's grasp because of the fact that many of the Rebels were wearing Union blue coats that they had captured at Glasgow. A large number of them had been taken just a couple days prior during the raid on Glasgow. All throughout the evening and into the night, the Union troops fought hard and were able to continue to drive the Confederates back. With their Spencer repeating rifles, the members of the Fourth Iowa Cavalry, which was part of Colonel Edward S. Winslow's brigade, took the lead. The amount of firepower that the Iowa troops were able to pour on the invaders was astonishing. In fact, the rifle fire was so intense that the Rebels completely withdrew and made their way back to their lines at the Blue River, where Marmaduke was preparing defenses that had been occupied by Blunt and his men just hours earlier. The rate of fire that the Union cavalry troopers possessed was, as mentioned earlier, a large factor in the battles to come, and the engagement between the Fourth Iowa and its Rebel foes was, in some way, a foreshadowing of this.

The opponents were finally settling in for the evening. Each side was preparing defenses and battle plans for the next day. Price knew that he was in dire circumstances at this point: Curtis's troops sat between him and the bounty in Kansas City, as well as the large supply of war matériel in Leavenworth. Not knowing exactly what the Army of the Border's strength was made it difficult to know what he was fighting. Additionally, these Kansas troops had put up a valiant effort. Price also knew that Pleasonton had his sights set on him and was pushing his rear elements to their limits. Price was essentially facing two armies, according to Kendall Gott. One was Curtis's command, and the other was Pleasonton's. Gott went on to say that, when discussing the impending battle called the Battle of Westport, Price's situation dictated that "he had to attack from the south. He was afraid of being forced north and getting pushed against the river," where he would be trapped and could be eliminated altogether. He needed to deal first with the army in front of him, Curtis's, and eliminate that as a threat. "He could then turn and face Pleasonton and eliminate [his army]." However, knowing the disposition of the large Federal units facing them, Price knew that he would have to abandon his plans to march into Kansas and get his immense wagon train out of the area as soon as was practical. At this point, he made the decision to turn his five hundred wagons south and head toward Little Santa Fe, which sat straight on the state line to the south. According to reports, "the slow-moving caravan was escorted by Tyler's brigade and Cabell's brigade, Price's largest and one of his best brigades." What this meant was that these two fine units, tasked with guarding Price's possessions, would be unavailable to fight in the upcoming battle and would dampen the hopes of a Rebel victory.

That evening, elements of Curtis's army began moving into position in a line that stretched from the north at Westport several miles south to an area just south of the old Shawnee Mission. The veterans of Lexington and Independence "mingled contemptuously with the militia who had remained timidly near the state line." Initially, Curtis ordered Blunt to move his troops back toward Kansas City after hearing news that Pleasonton had indeed reached Price and had engaged him. Blunt was reluctant to do this and pled his case to keep his troops in a line to the east of Westport, which they did. Additionally, the militia troops under Deitzler were pulled from their positions on the northern section of the Big Blue River and inserted by Curtis and Blunt as a reserve south of Kansas City. The Kansas militiamen were anything but seasoned soldiers. Most had seen little combat, and among those who had tasted it were those who had seen the horror of the Bleeding Kansas days. The fact that many of these troops had never faced down Confederate guns was certainly one of the unknowns of this engagement. The defenses were set, and the two armies were poised to face each other in a battle that has often been referred to as the "Gettysburg of the West." It was destined to become the largest battle fought west of the Mississippi River during the entire war.

October 23 dawned a cool and clear morning. The Confederates were arrayed with two divisions, Shelby's and Fagan's, facing off against the Union forces entrenched to their north. Marmaduke assumed a defensive posture around Byram's Ford and faced directly at General Pleasonton's troopers, who were massed to his east. Marmaduke's division was to play a crucial role in the action of the day. If it could delay and perhaps destroy Pleasonton's force, Shelby and Fagan could roll over the untested militia and allow the expedition to continue south—and perhaps escape to friendly territory and fight another day. Marmaduke was outnumbered, however. He was facing three of Pleasonton's brigades, led by Sanborn, Winslow and Phillips, that totaled about 3,500 well-armed Union troopers. Marmaduke's command numbered only about 2,700, but they were well entrenched and had every chance of driving the men in blue back from the Blue River.

Phillips's brigade dismounted his cavalrymen, as was often typical of cavalry troops, and began to advance on the Rebel positions. Between Phillips's men and the Confederate positions lay the Blue River and then an open field that they would need to move across to continue the attack. The Rebels answered the charge with an immense amount of fire, which stopped Phillips's advance in its tracks. "Balls from Marmaduke's men chipped the leafless trees around his advancing men." Yet they continued their advance until the fire became so intense that they had to stop or face annihilation. A short time passed, with shots being traded between the two forces and with Phillips's brigade brought to a grinding halt. Sanborn's and Winslow's men finally came forward to aid in the advance against Marmaduke. With the extra weight of their brigades, the Union troops were able to dislodge the Rebels from their positions. Marmaduke was driven farther west toward Kansas, pursued by Pleasonton's fierce cavalry, many units of which had gotten back on their mounts and continued slamming into the Rebels vigorously.

Meanwhile, a future hero emerged from the shadows. Wounded severely, Colonel Winslow had to be relieved of his command. In his place would be a man who would lead the charge at Mine Creek and later serve with Custer at Little Bighorn. Lieutenant Colonel Frederick Benteen was born and raised in Baltimore but moved to St. Louis when he was fifteen. He was currently the commander of the Tenth Missouri Cavalry and was an aggressive, hard-riding and capable commander who was ready to take the fight to the Rebels. The cavalry, having completed its objective and having pushed Marmaduke's troopers back to the west, continued pushing until those men were effectively out of the fight:

> *The victorious Union Missourians looked west across the rolling tableland between the Big Blue and the Kansas state line. Toward the south, stone fences crosshatched the farmsteads, and a brick mansion with white*

> *pillars—the "Wornall House"—stood by a road running north to Kansas City. In the fields to the west and south as far as the Federals could see stood Price's army...As the Union soldiers gazed with wonder, Pleasonton rode up under his general's flag and watched. Pointing at the distant figures, he shouted, "Rebels, rebels, rebels, fire, fire, you damned asses."*

Meanwhile, on the north end of the battlefield, as Pleasonton's men were clashing with Marmaduke's charges and driving them out of their positions, Curtis's men were well positioned and ready for the Rebel charge. "Blunt's division was moved from Westport to Brush Creek, which runs through what is known as the Country Club Plaza in Kansas City, beneath a high hill," which was situated on the southern side. The Federals had a number of artillery pieces and entrenchments to check the Confederate advance. They also had a numerical superiority over Shelby's and Fagan's men, remembering that part of Fagan's division—the one led by Brigadier General Cabell, who was considered to be "a very competent and aggressive officer"—had been pulled away to guard the wagon train, which had, by this time, become an absolute albatross hanging around Price's neck. The brigade of Kansans under Moonlight, which had shown that it could stand against the Rebels, was placed to the west of this flank as insurance against a breakthrough and advance into Kansas:

> *Anticipating Price's impending attack, Blunt had positioned his three available brigades along Brush Creek, while a fourth under Colonel Charles Blair was en route from Kansas City. East of Wornall Lane was the brigade of J. Hobart Ford. West of Wornall was the brigade of Charles "Doc" Jennison, with an artillery battery in support. Two regiments of cavalry filled the gap to the west between Jennison and the Kansas/Missouri state line.*

The Confederates charged. The Union gunners opened fire. The Rebels marched down the bluff facing Brush Creek but were unable to carry the field, as their opponents fought intensely and pushed them back. While being pushed back, they reached elements of Marmaduke's division, which had been routed by Pleasonton's troopers. Shelby attempted a charge at Moonlight's and Jennison's brigades and was successful in driving both back considerably from their original positions. Moonlight retreated across the state line back into Kansas, and Jennison was pushed back north to Westport. Reinforced, the Federals continued a back-and-forth battle with Shelby's and Fagan's men that ranged from north to south. Shelby's men continued to push against the stubborn resistance of the Kansans. Eventually, the weight of the Union advance, the fact that Shelby's men were running low on ammunition and the fact that he had been ordered to give support to Marmaduke's men, who were under intense pressure, caused Shelby to be pushed back south a couple of miles toward the Wornall House. There he was able to make a stand, with many of his men finding excellent cover from which to hold off the Federal troopers, who were charging hard at them, swelled by the pride of the victory they had just experienced.

Here Shelby awaited the remainder of Price's forces, who were moving as fast as they could to the south. The hard fighting of Shelby was a particularly fine example of his ability as a field commander. His division had just been pivotal in helping Price escape from certain defeat by holding off the Union advance and allowing the massive wagon train to stream its way south. It was now headed straight south along the Fort Leavenworth–Fort Gibson road toward Arkansas. As the Confederate forces were falling apart and retreating out of the Kansas City area, Shelby retreated with them. Many reports of massive prairie grass fires were thought to have been set by the Rebels to cover their retreat, and the area was said to be widely strewn with dead and wounded men, battle implements and personal possessions that had been tossed aside as the army had made its rapid advance south.

The Union forces pushed southward behind the retreating Army of Missouri, making certain that it was leaving the area. At this critical juncture, in a farmhouse situated ten miles south of Westport, the Union commanders gathered. Here they would make the fateful decisions that would affect the rest of the campaign. They decided that the pursuit of

A painting of the Battle of Westport, Missouri, October 23, 1864, by N.C. Wyeth. *Courtesy of the Missouri State Historical Society.*

An engraving of cavalry action, published by *Harper's Weekly. Author's collection.*

Price was their shared goal and wanted to completely destroy his forces and remove him from Kansas completely. It was, however, not a popular decision with all of the commanders present. Pleasonton wanted nothing to do with a march through southern Kansas. His main goal was to get out of Kansas and back to St. Louis. His argument centered on the fact that he felt that Curtis needed no more men and equipment to destroy Price and that his men had been in constant pursuit for the better part of a month and were completely exhausted. This argument did not sit well with Carney and Deitzler, however. They felt very strongly that the Kansas militiamen should be allowed to return to their homes before the "regular troops" should be released. Generals Curtis and Blunt were also in favor of this because the militia had done what they were tasked with doing: they had pushed back at Price's army and saved Leavenworth, Lawrence and the rest of northern Kansas from certain invasion.

With that, Curtis sent a memo that ended martial law for the northern Kansas area and sent the warriors, now battle veterans who had helped save their state, back to their homes. He did, however, keep martial law in effect for the southern areas of Kansas and retained the troops from those counties and areas through which Price's army was headed. Price's army had been defeated, but he was allowed to slip through the hands of the Union forces and was still largely intact. They would go on to fight another day very soon. The "Gettysburg of the West" had ended. The Battle of Westport saw nearly 30,000 combatants square off on the very ground that would become the city of Kansas City. Roughly 1,500 men on each side became casualties of the Battle of Westport. The border between Kansas and Missouri was safely in Union control, never to be threatened again during the entire War Between the States.

Chapter 4

Retreat from Kansas City

By the time the sun rose on October 24, the Battle of Westport was a memory. It had been brutal for both sides, and now the Rebels wanted to get home. The battles of the Missouri Campaign that rolled through the state of Missouri in September and October had taken a toll on both sides. Constant attacks, skirmishes, retreats and pursuits had worn down these thousands of men. Westport really sealed the need, exceedingly apparent to Price, that his Confederate army must make haste and get out of Union territory as soon as possible. Price was, however, unwavering in his desire to move his massive train of wagons filled with the plunder of the long campaign, including arms, personal possessions, cattle, gold, ammunition and more. Nearly anything that wasn't nailed down was picked up by Price's men and hauled off. St. Louis and Jefferson City had been abandoned. The pro-Union government still reigned in Jefferson City, and Leavenworth became impossible as a target because of the crushing defeat at Westport. This wagon train represented, at this late stage of the campaign, the only tangible evidence that the march through Missouri had experienced any modicum of success. Despite pleas from many of his subordinates, Price was determined to keep moving with this wagon if for no other reason but to justify his existence.

The beaten, beleaguered and bedraggled Confederate wagon train and men snaked their way down the Kansas/Missouri state line, dejected and eager to just get home to friendly territory. All along the way, broken wagons, blankets, arms, boxes, tack, trash, rifles and anything undesirable to the rank and file Rebel soldier was tossed aside. The wagon train stretched for miles and was extremely slow due to several factors, including the fact that many were pulled by oxen and that Price, as mentioned earlier, was a former infantry commander who, according to Gott, "wasn't pushing his guys." Additionally, after a major battle, it is simply difficult to recover that quickly from the sheer exhaustion that comes from exerting oneself to such an incredible level. This mess made the Rebel army easy to track. The road south was also desolate: "Here and there were stark chimneys of burned houses—called by Missourians 'Jennison's monuments.'"

During the evening of the twenty-third, the Confederate army made it several miles south and camped for the night. When Colonel Moonlight's men reached the small town of Aubrey, they were able to see the fires that were burning in the Rebel camp glowing in the night. Moonlight was to keep at a distance during the twenty-fourth and twenty-fifth along the right side of Price's army to guard against Price's men raiding the towns along the way that lay to the west of the column. Moonlight's men were charged with keeping Price moving south along the state line and seeing to it that he made no turn into Kansas.

The morning of the twenty-fourth found the Rebels on the move again. A few miles behind them marched Curtis's Union force, the Army of the Border, made up of Blunt's troopers, who were in the lead, and Pleasonton's cavalry, which was bringing up the rear. Blunt's division consisted of four

A cavalry sketch by war correspondent Winslow Homer. *Author's collection.*

separate brigades commanded by Colonel Moonlight, Colonel Jennison, Colonel James Ford and Colonel Charles Blair. The total strength for this division is estimated to be nearly 2,500 men split between the four regiments. Moonlight's regiment had about 750 men, Jennison's was about 900; the other two are harder to factor simply because many of the militia would simply leave the formation during the long march south as soon as they were near to their homes. This meant not just individual men walking away but also large units, including those as large as whole regiments. These units and men were near their homes, and they felt they had done their jobs.

Moreover, these were not regular troops who had received a great amount of training. They were, for the most part, local men who were farmers, bankers or blacksmiths who had heeded Governor Carney's call to arms. It was truly a "citizen army" if ever there was one. Without the regular training that army units underwent, it is easy to see why these units might not have had the willingness or ability to even keep up with the trained troops and to move forward with the army as it trailed Price. These factors led to a mass exodus in many of the units and an inability to really pinpoint what the total strength of Blunt's division truly was on the twenty-fourth and twenty-fifth.

Behind Blunt's division rode General Pleasonton and the second division, which was made up of regular volunteer units, as well as the Missouri Enrolled Militia and the Missouri State Militia mentioned earlier. Pleasonton's force was twice as large as Blunt's, with a combined strength of well over 5,000 men. These men were the ones who had crumbled Marmaduke's division at Westport and were riding hard to finish the job that had eluded them when Price was allowed to escape. Also part of the larger force, serving directly under General Curtis's command, were elements of the Eleventh Kansas Cavalry and the Second Kansas Cavalry, along with "36 artillery pieces; 16 being rifled guns, the other 20 being the short range mountain howitzers." In total, Curtis's command was somewhere in the neighborhood of 8,000 men, and there was a significant amount of artillery support to go along with it. In addition to the 8,000 in Curtis's column, you can add Moonlight's 750 men, who were out in the field to the west shadowing Price's column, although this group was too far away to really effect change and would not be directly involved in the fighting in the next couple of days. Moonlight was also continuing to add men from the local counties as he marched, ever vigilant for any groups to break away from the Army of Missouri and begin wreaking havoc on the cities along and west of the Missouri/Kansas border.

The Confederates were able to reform to a great degree and were back largely in their particular divisions led by Marmaduke, Shelby and

Fagan. At this point of the campaign, Price's army still had an effective strength of about twelve thousand men, with an additional three thousand unarmed men. This is roughly the same number of men Price had when he crossed the border into Missouri in early September. Many men had been killed, wounded and captured in the march through Missouri, which had culminated thus far at the Battle of Westport. Pilot Knob and Westport saw significant casualties, which really hampered Confederate fighting ability.

Through it all, Price had the good fortune to be able to recruit heavily along the way. These new men were pressed into the army and interspersed throughout the divisions. These divisions still shaped up to be a formidable force, with Marmaduke commanding 2,700 armed men, Fagan 4,500 armed men and Shelby almost 4,500 armed men. In addition to the nearly 12,000 armed men were the 3,000 unarmed men under the command of Colonel Charles Taylor. Despite the heavy casualties, recruitments brought upward of 5,000 armed and unarmed men. A major issue with this was that many of these troops who were thrown into the divisions were untrained and undisciplined troops with no combat experience. Much like the Kansas men who were thrown into the lines at Westport, there was no way to predict how they would react in a combat experience.

Despite what many had faced at Westport or even earlier at Pilot Knob, this was, in many ways, a fairly unseasoned army. The army that was bearing down on them, especially in Pleasonton's case, was a more professional and better-armed force than they had seen before. These troops were now beaten and retreating into Kansas. They would, in less than a day, be asked to face off against a seasoned and well-armed cavalry force that was "flushed with their triumph and ready for additional punishment of the Confederates," despite their horses being tired or jaded and the fact that many had eaten very little in the last few days and had rested almost no time at all. They had been in hot pursuit for days. Most of the rank and file knew that they could attack them now and wouldn't have to see them again. In other words, they just wanted to be done with it, get their revenge on the Missourians and get them out of their state once and for all. Having said that, the sheer exhaustion of both man and beast contributed to the slow pursuit of the Rebels and really allowed this army to escape the grasp of the Union forces and remain largely intact, despite the defeat handed to the men. The Confederate soldier in the field, however, was looking at it a bit differently. He was done with the campaign and simply wanted to get home. This wasn't a totally demoralized army, however. In fact, it is said that Price's army remained in fairly high spirits despite the defeat at Westport.

One thing had to be certain as the Rebels sat in their encampment the evening of the twenty-third after they had taken a severe beating earlier that day at the hands of Curtis's army: they were done. They were tired, weary, broken, injured, hungry and ready to get away from hated Kansas and all that it stood for. The road out of Kansas ran along the Kansas/Missouri border in a north–south line from Fort Leavenworth all the way south into Indian Territory, what is today Oklahoma, and to Fort Gibson. The majority of the road wound its way down through Kansas, but a significant portion of it broke just across the Missouri border, ending up back in Kansas somewhere near the settlement of Trading Post. The Army of Missouri camped that night in its namesake state fully aware of the fact that it was in a perilous position. The troopers knew that the Army of the Border was on their heels but that they were some distance off. They were also cognizant of the fact that they had narrowly averted disaster at Westport when the Union troops were slow to react after their victory. General Shelby had fought a brilliant rear guard action, allowing the bulk of the army to safely retreat.

What was to come of this campaign now? If they were allowed to divest themselves of this slow-moving train and make rapidly out of the state, the Union troops would have no real ability to catch them. They could make their way to Fort Scott, capture the stores there, refit the army and be on their way safely out of Kansas. Price would not acquiesce. There was no way that he would release his wagons, the only tangible sign of success for this entire campaign, and run away. The Confederates would need to summon the courage to fight off the Federals; in the next two days, the army only covered thirty-four and twenty-eight miles respectively. This was not a breakneck pace, and it was not only viewed as too slow for a cavalry retreat, but it was also seen as a fairly slow retreat even for an infantry march. What the army needed to do was pick up the pace and put miles between them and the Union cavalry. Lumir Buresh surmised that with "a rapid movement of 40–50 miles a day, it would not have been possible for the Federals to catch them." Remember that the Union command took valuable time to debate what the next move would be after the Battle of Westport had been decided.

After a rest on the night of the twenty-third, Price and his column mounted up and determined to continue their retreat. This became a monumental task because of the sheer size of the wagon train. Horses, men, wagons, cattle, prisoners and artillery caissons all had to be formed up and made into a force capable of both making time and dealing with the threat behind them. This inability to organize properly was another Rebel fault that allowed the Union forces precious time to organize themselves, chew up valuable miles, and make up lost time in their pursuit. The Confederates marched on into the desolate prairie south along the state line. Unlike the eastern Kansas/ western Missouri of today, with its beautiful grass, hills, cities and multitude of trees, it was nearly devoid of all vegetation, with the exception of the rolling hills covered with prairie bluestem grasses, some of which were as high as a man.

The band continued on as the road wound through the Missouri side of the state line, which was even more desolate than the Kansas side. Remembering Thomas Ewing, the hero of Pilot Knob, and his issuance of Order 11, the Missouri troops surely held this close in the front of their minds and had to be seeking revenge for this. There was nothing. Ewing had seen to that. Everyone was forced from the area unless they could somehow prove their allegiance to the Union. Families from as far north as Kansas City and as far south as Nevada were ripped from their homes and forcibly removed from the border counties. This was not, however, an arbitrary decision, and many Missourians surely walked with blood on their hands. Order 11 was issued on August 25, 1863, just four days removed from William Quantrill's raid on Lawrence in which nearly two hundred people were killed in cold blood by Quantrill and his border ruffians.

An engraving of Quantrill's raid on Lawrence, published in *Harper's Weekly. Author's collection.*

Onward the huge column marched until it crossed back into Kansas. Eastern Kansas, untouched by Order 11, was vibrant with farms, families, towns and crops in the field. Here is where the Army of Missouri began to exact some amount of revenge. Crops, homes, haystacks and barns were burned. Food, cattle, personal property and anything that caught the eye of one of the invaders was fair game for confiscation. People were also being killed by the raiders. When the lead elements of Curtis's army came upon Trading Post, "the advance guard found the body of an elderly preacher lying in a field, shot by some of Price's men…his cabin plundered and afire. A dead horse had been dumped into the well. The Confederates had robbed and murdered three other settlers in the neighborhood and shot at several more." Among Shelby's Missourians rode many bushwhackers who were certainly eager for revenge. They had fought against the abolitionists for years and had seen their way of life threatened, according to Major John N. Edwards, Shelby's chief of staff:

> *Shelby was soothing the wounds of Missouri by stabbing the breast of Kansas…He was fighting the devil with fire and smoking him to death. Haystacks, houses, barns, produce, crops, and farming implements were consumed before the march of his squadrons, and what flames spared the bullet finished.*

The Rebel army arrived at Trading Post later that evening on the twenty-fourth and set up its camp. The men immediately set out into the countryside, foraging for food and supplies, preparing some of the cattle, which were being killed to feed the Rebel troops who, by this time, were extremely hungry. The local residents were in fear of the Rebel raiders and lost most of the food that they had stored up to them. The invaders entered private homes and took all food off their shelves. The locals found that nothing at all was sacred. Homes were ransacked, crops in the field were stolen to feed the men and livestock was liberated to also turn into food for the Rebel invaders.

On the morning of the twenty-fourth, the men of the Army of the Border departed their encampment at Little Santa Fe and headed in pursuit of the Rebels. As previously noted, Moonlight's men camped fifteen miles south at Aubrey in sight of the Rebel campfires. When Moonlight sighted the Rebel army beginning to stir, he ordered his men up and departed. Moonlight was under orders to protect the right flank and keep Price's forces at bay in case they made a turn toward the interior of Kansas or sent bands of marauders into the countryside to threaten the small towns along the Kansas border. Moonlight followed these orders to the letter, even at the risk of the welfare of his men and horses, as there was little forage available. Colonel Thomas Moonlight was an astute soldier bent on protecting Kansas as much as possible.

It became very clear that Price was going to continue along the Leavenworth/Fort Gibson road, which would take them directly toward Trading Post and, farther to the southeast, Mound City. Along the way to Mound City, Moonlight was able to add to his troop totals when he ran across the Eleventh Kansas Militia, which had 300 men at Coldwater Grove. Extremely early in the morning of the twenty-fifth, Moonlight reached his destination and found Mound City safe. Moonlight's troop totals began to swell even more when several detachments of the Kansas Militia arrived to aid in the defense of Mound City. Moonlight was looking at about 1,600 men under arms. This was a small force that would have a tough time against a true concerted effort to dislodge it from the town and capture its military supplies. The town was also thought to be a possible Rebel target due to the fact that this was the home of the hated Doc Jennison and was a gathering place for Jayhawkers, who regularly raided across the state line into Missouri.

In the meantime, the main body of the Union forces was preparing to move out but was not making good progress at all. The troops were tired and their horses were worn out. One other possible explanation for such a late start could simply have been the fact that all three of the commanding generals were worn out and not ready to get started without proper rest and that they knew that their men and horses were also completely worn down. The late start caused a great amount of delay for the Union troops and precluded them from getting to within striking distance of Price's rear elements until very late on the twenty-fourth and with no time to reconnoiter the area, which would have seriously hampered Curtis's ability to formulate a rational battle plan. The first of Blunt's troops moved out possibly at about 8:00 a.m., with the last elements of Pleasonton's cavalry not getting underway until about 10:00 a.m. Blunt's men were in the vanguard of the army, and Pleasonton's followed behind. Along the way, the debris of the Rebel army was everywhere. It was not a difficult army to track, as mentioned.

The damp ground was churned and the wasted equipment, matériel and broken wagons fairly littered the landscape. There were also a fair number of Price's men who were too exhausted to move any further or were too wounded or sick to continue with the army. These men just lay along the road awaiting capture by the pursuing Union soldiers. The army reached

West Point, which was about nine miles away from Trading Post, just as the sky was beginning to darken at about 6:00 p.m. There Blunt's men found that Price's army had left a great amount of food supplies behind in their hasty retreat. This was welcome news for the hungry boys in blue, who had been on the march all day. Here the men of Blunt's tired division sat, rested and awaited Pleasonton's division, which was led by Pleasonton and Curtis. Pleasonton's division arrived a couple of hours behind Blunt's and was ordered to replace Blunt's division at the front of the column after a two-hour halt in the march. The fact that Curtis replaced Blunt's division with Pleasonton's in the front of the army was a point of contention for Blunt. There were a great many political entanglements and a great deal of strife amongst the Kansas men, who were due for a large election only two weeks hence. Senator James Lane was traveling with the forces and was especially close to General Blunt, whom Lane had aided in securing a general's star for him. This meant that the two men were very close.

General Curtis, however, had found himself as head of the Department of Kansas because he had failed to play a good political game as the head of the Department of Missouri and was relegated to Kansas. As in Missouri, Curtis was simply unable to deal effectively with any of the local politicians. The replacement of Blunt's division in the lead of the army did not, for obvious reasons, sit well with Senator Lane, who wanted to be seen as an integral part of a successful campaign against Price to help bolster his résumé to the voters and win reelection as senator. Kansas governor Carney was, however, supporting another man for Lane's seat. The political capital for Lane could be great. As could the spoils for another political figure who was fighting with the Army of the Border: Colonel Samuel Crawford, who happened to be running for governor against Carney. This all made for sticky footing for the Union command.

Blunt, who was a generally fiery and aggressive commander, had suggested pushing his division on that evening to the south end of Price's army and attempting to outflank him. He would then be in position to hit Price early the next morning. The issue with an assault led by Blunt's division on the large Confederate force was that it was simply too small to have any success in a frontal attack. Price, due to slow reaction after the Battle of Westport, had escaped from the Federals with most of his army intact and still had the capability of defeating this Union force. Curtis balked at Blunt's suggestion that they attempt to move the entire army across the Marais des Cygnes River that night. That way, their forces would be in position for an immediate attack the next morning and would not have to make the crossing under the

An engraving of cavalry riding, published in *Harper's Weekly*. *Author's collection.*

guns of the Rebels. It was instead Curtis's decision that the entire army would continue to advance on the Rebels and attack in force. Curtis also upheld his order that Pleasonton's cavalry would lead the pursuit.

General Curtis finally got word that some of his elements, the Second Colorado Cavalry, had already been engaged with the Rebel pickets. General Blunt was unable to provide support, so the Colorado troopers withdrew from the area and took up positions near the "mounds." The mounds were two hills that the road led directly through. The mound on the east was about 130 feet high, and the one on the west side of the road rose about 150 feet. They were two rather imposing features on a land that was generally devoid of large natural landmarks. Curtis was excited to hear this information. He tasked General Sanborn with leading the advance on Trading Post—General Pleasonton claimed to be too sick to lead it himself. Sanborn departed immediately with his own brigade, as well as elements of Benteen's brigade, the Fourth Iowa Veteran Volunteer Cavalry. Sanborn's troops reached the mounds. He deployed his forces and prepared to attack. More skirmishing occurred, and many of the Confederate pickets fell under the fire from the Union guns. Unfortunately, it was a dark night, and a thunderstorm had moved into the area. Lightning streaked across the sky, and thunder echoed through the prairie. Sanborn did not want to risk hitting enemies he could not see, was not certain where they were located and also was not familiar with the ground, so he wisely broke off the attack and decided to wait for morning light.

The disposition of the Union troops was difficult at best. They were spread in a line that stretched from Sanborn's headquarters, which he established about "three miles north of the mounds," to Blunt's division, which sat five miles away in West Point. The night was miserable for the troopers as the rain and thunder continued. It was also late October in Kansas, which meant that it was cold. Throughout the miserable night the Army of the Border waited for the chance to move out and destroy Price's Army of Missouri and force it from Kansas.

Chapter 5

Trading Post and Marais des Cygnes

October 25 was a fateful day for both armies. Major General Sterling Price was desperate to escape Kansas with his huge wagon train intact to have tangible evidence of a successful foray into Missouri and Kansas. Major General Samuel Curtis was also on his own mission: to destroy the Confederate army and send it out of Kansas for good. Early that morning, General Sanborn had made contact with the enemy but had halted his advance due to his perception that the Rebels were in force opposite him and that it was too dark to make an attack on the mounds that night. He felt that it would be much more sensible to do it in the light. Curtis, however, could smell victory and sent a message to General Sanborn that he was to attack anyway. He instructed him to use artillery support and take control of the position by daylight.

Others suggested alternate means of taking the position and destroying the Rebel army, including a flanking maneuver that would effectively cut the enemy off from escape and destroy them en masse. Curtis was unwavering and carried on with the planned attack led by Sanborn, who was in the process of preparing for it. He placed his two batteries of guns within range of the Rebel positions and prepared to open fire. Sanborn had at his disposal well under one thousand men, whereas the Confederate rear guard exceeded well over two thousand and also had two guns to provide artillery support. Sanborn's plan called for a dismounted charge, with the two forces split and attacking different mounds. Sanborn used his Fourth Iowa Cavalry, his Second Colorado Cavalry and the Sixth and Eighth Missouri State Militia to lead the attack.

The first stages of the attack began just before the gray skies shed their first light. The Confederate pickets were quickly overwhelmed at the base of the mound and were driven back toward their lines. They continued their attack and began to drive the enemy back in rapid fashion to the edge of the Marais des Cygnes River, which ran just to the south of the two mounds. Initially, the attackers of the Second Colorado had their way with the Rebels, but they were eventually forced back by the Rebel defenders, although they were able to take a number of prisoners. The artillery pieces also began to shake the ground around the mounds as soon as they were positioned and were able to train their guns on the defenders. The Fourth Iowa and the Missouri State Militia were also beginning their push against their intended targets. They moved rapidly to the mound and took the top with little difficulty as they had a great deal of cover to protect their advance. Remember that the mound was covered with large rocks and timber. When they reached the summit of the west mound, they were able to easily make out the Rebel army retreating into the distance.

The artillery, meanwhile, was firing on the east mound as the Sixth and Eighth Missouri State Militias were preparing their assaults on it. The artillery shells, while not overly effective in clearing the Rebels from the mound, most certainly were able to get the army moving, as many of the shells sailed over the mound, at their half-mile distance, and made a rapid move out of the area a priority for the defenders. The east mound, with its far more sparse cover and the brunt of the enemy force, about two thousand men, was a bit more daunting of a task. The Rebels opened fire with their small guns, and the Union gunners, with their more substantial batteries, then began to return the fire on the Confederate guns and quickly silenced them. It is reported that, given the nature of the placement of the guns and the height of the mound, the Rebels were almost completely unable to lay down an effective base of fire on the advancing Federal troops.

The mound also had a very steep curve at its base, which helped to shield the attackers and allowed them to reach the base without being detected, let alone be pushed back. When the Missouri State Militia members reached the base, they began their ascent up the steep face of the hill, which was an arduous process. They were eventually able to reach the summit and prepared to charge the large force of defenders only to discover that they were not on the hill any longer. Cabell, most likely sensing that he could easily be cut off from an escape by the Union forces moving around to the west side of the mounds, decided that he needed to take the opportunity to move off the hill and rejoin the rest of the army. Other elements of Sanborn's force took up the chase and pushed the defenders back to the river, where Price was endeavoring to make a crossing at the nearest ford on the Marais de Cygnes and escape once again.

Not having a force sufficient to take on the large Confederate army, Sanborn's men broke off their pursuit. This was not before the Second Arkansas was able to secure the capture of two of Price's guns, which were most likely the guns that had a short time earlier been firing on the Union troops. The Union troops then began surveying the area that had been the Rebel camp. They captured, in addition to the guns, about one hundred prisoners, many wagons and a great deal of livestock that had to be abandoned by the enemy troopers as they beat a hasty retreat. All around them they found the signs of a force completely taken by surprise and compelled to get underway as soon as possible: fires with meat still smoking on the spits, water still boiling and equipment and personal possessions laying all over—it was reported that "the stench of the entire area was nearly suffocating."

This small battle was the first action of essentially a daylong rolling battle that stretched all the way from Trading Post to Fort Scott and involved several different skirmishes, of which the Battle of Mine Creek was the watershed

A lithograph by Samuel R. Reading of Confederates retreating through Linn County, Missouri. *Author's collection.*

event of the day. Casualties were light in the action for both armies. This was certainly by no means a major battle in terms of the Missouri Campaign, but it did have an impact in several ways. According to Kendall Gott, "This should have alerted Price that the Union force was nearby" and was prepared to finish the battle, but it did little in the way of slowing the Union army. Additionally, although it held "no real strategic impact, it certainly alerted the Union command that there was a rear guard."

Pleasonton could see the Confederate army streaming to the south for miles, with the road churned to mud. Sanborn, under orders from General Pleasonton, was given control of the majority of his division and tasked with effecting a river crossing and continuing the pursuit of Price. All the while harassed by Rebel skirmishers, the Union troops slowly crossed the ford and began to form up on the other side. The crossing was made extremely difficult due to the fact that a tributary stream called Big Sugar Creek also had to be negotiated. Along the ford, the Rebels had chopped down trees to block it and had well-placed snipers who rained nuisance fire on the troops trying to cross. It was becoming apparent that the Rebels would not go quietly and would attempt to put up at least token resistance the entire route. They had to, after all, protect Price's precious wagons and allow the Army of Missouri to continue its advance south.

Once the forward elements had crossed, other units began to make their way across as well. Driving the skirmishers back steadily and rooting out the straggling snipers took time, however, and the Rebels were able to form up again and make a new line of battle to continue to delay Pleasonton's men. Marmaduke detached Clark's brigade to make a stand just to the south of the river. Also in the line facing the Union troopers were three artillery pieces. The Union Second Arkansas Cavalry, led by Colonel John F. Phelps, came upon this skirmish line and soon found itself being attacked from the line of the Rebels with artillery and small arms bearing down on Phelps's men and placing them under heavy pressure. Phelps and his men were reluctantly forced to retreat out of range of the guns. Despite a tremendous amount of pressure from Curtis, the Union troops, under Pleasonton's orders, waited for some time for additional support, including artillery, before Pleasonton would continue the charge. This, again, gave Price additional time to put more distance between his precious wagons and the advancing Union forces. Ultimately, Pleasonton's forces were ready to begin the charge. As they began forward, Clark began a hasty withdrawal, as well took two of his three guns with him.

During this time, the two regiments that Clark detached from his brigade, those of Burbridge and Greene, had been ordered to move farther south and form another line of battle. As Clark withdrew his men to this fallback position, they took their place with them. Clark now had his entire brigade and artillery support intact and prepared to make a stand. Colonel John Phillips and his brigade, followed shortly by Lieutenant Colonel Frederick Benteen, had been riding hard to the south. Benteen had been riding all night and had taken no time to forage for food, and his horses and men were near the point of exhaustion (see his after-action report in the final chapter). Clark and his brigade now faced an effective force of three brigades—Sanborn's, Benteen's and Phillips's—that totaled 3,500 men. Sanborn was also able to bring two artillery pieces to bear that, at a distance, traded shots with Clark's batteries. Sanborn assembled his line of battle, placing Lieutenant Colonel Benteen's brigade in the center of the attack, with Colonel Phillips's brigade and Sanborn's own brigade providing flank support on either side of Benteen. They readied for the charge, obviously representing an impressive group against the small Rebel force. As with Clark's initial defense, he thought better of facing a charge of 3,500 Union cavalrymen and galloped off to the south with his force intact.

With that, the fighting at the Marais des Cygnes came to an end. There were few casualties, but this line of skirmishes did have an impact on the day. It continued to delay Curtis's Army of the Border and allowed valuable time for Price to continue his retreat to the south. Price and his army continued south. He could be trailed easily by the ruts in the morass of the road and by the endless amount of discarded items and broken wagons. By now, Price realized that he was in a critical situation. He must do something to stop the Union army and get out of Kansas in some semblance of order. The rear guard action had been fairly successful up until this point since the army had made it about halfway down the Kansas/Missouri state line and was still intact. At this point, he made the decision to double his rear guard, which to that point had been handled by Fagan's division. He now halted Marmaduke's division and placed it in the rear of the column to serve as the new rear guard, with Fagan's division marching just in front of Marmaduke's and ready to serve as a reserve in case Marmaduke needed aid. The remainder of Price's train would be escorted by Shelby and his men, who would be ready to raid Fort Scott and secure the rumored vast supply of arms and equipment there. Price hoped against hope that he would be able to make it to Fort Scott and that his two rear divisions could hold off the Federals long enough to get him out of the state of Kansas.

Chapter 6

"Charge With Me, for God's Sake!"

Colonel Sanborn, Lieutenant Colonel Benteen and Colonel Phillips continued their advance south with their brigades, trailing the Rebels as they went. As mentioned, it was not a difficult task to keep the enemy within striking distance. Sanborn had been up since late the night before and had been involved in the fighting at the mounds and at Marais des Cygnes, and his troops were exhausted. They fell out of the column a few miles south of the Marais des Cygnes so that they could feed their tired horses, as well as themselves. Phillips led the way and Benteen followed until they reached a major fork in the road about three miles beyond the spot where they had left Sanborn's brigade. This is a major intersection in terms of the eastern section of Kansas, with roads that led to Mound City, where Moonlight's men had moved to the night before, and the other two forks were the two roads to Fort Scott, one east of the other running parallel to the south.

Price had chosen to take the Fort Scott road instead of sticking to the military road, and Phillips followed him. Benteen took the other road, which ran east of the fork that Phillips had taken. At about 11:00 a.m. that morning, Phillips and his Missouri State Militia found what they had been looking for. The Rebel army was in battle formation on the north side of Mine Creek and was supported by artillery. Phillips, without hesitation, put his men to work forming their own battle line. Lieutenant Colonel Bazel Lazear and his First Missouri State Militia, which was leading Phillips's advance, pushed the waiting Rebel picket men back south toward Mine Creek with very little effort. At this point, all of Phillips's men were set for battle. Lazear's men were met with a rapid succession of volleys from the Confederate ranks, at which point Lazear prepared his men by dismounting them and forming them in a line as per standard Union cavalry doctrine.

Benteen also arrived on the battlefield at about the same time. His troops, as stated in his after-action report, were in line as follows: "First, the Tenth Missouri Cavalry, Maj. W.H. Lusk; second, the Fourth Iowa Cavalry, Maj. A.R. Pierce; third, the Third Iowa Cavalry, Maj. B.S. Jones, and fourth, the Seventh Indiana Cavalry and Fourth Missouri Cavalry, consolidated, under the command of Major S.E.W. Simonson, of the former regiment." As he reached the summit of the slight rise of the land, which slopes gently down toward Mine Creek, he took stock of the situation. In front of him was a Rebel force much larger than one he and Phillips could muster. Between the two brigades of Benteen and Phillips, there were about 2,700 men staring at about 7,000 Confederate troopers.

At this point of the battle, Phillips and his brigade were situated about a mile north of the edge of Mine Creek. Benteen and his brigade were formed to his immediate left. Between the two brigades ran the Fort Scott road, which sloped down the hill toward the middle of the Rebel lines and ran to the ford at the creek. The land around was a gently rolling prairie with very few, if any, trees in sight. You could literally see for miles in any direction. Lieutenant Colonel Benteen stated in his

Union lieutenant colonel Frederick Benteen. *Courtesy of the Kansas State Historical Society.*

Union colonel John F. Phillips. *Courtesy of the Kansas State Historical Society.*

report that "the skies now cleared, and the sun smiled out upon the scene as if foretelling the glorious day that awaited us." This ground was also perfect for a cavalry charge.

Mine Creek was, by this time, completely choked with wagons trying in vain to get across the ford. The ford itself was a good one, with a rock bottom, but it had a steep bank on the south side of it. You had to take a wagon into the ford and then jog slightly before going up the other side. It was also a fairly cold day, and the banks of the creek were awash with mud from the previous day's rains. This ford, along with the rest of the military road, was often used by typically no more than twenty or thirty wagons in a standard military train, not the hundreds that Price attempted to push through, so the creek was a quagmire on both sides. By the time Phillips and Benteen rode up, the wagon train was only about 80 percent complete with its crossing. There were still about one hundred wagons that had not been able to navigate the narrow ford. Price was also, along with Shelby, quite a distance down the road when the battle lines began to form.

Marmaduke and his men were in a serious situation. The wagon train was not clear of the ford, and something needed to be done. He had originally felt that he would have time to establish a strong defensive position on the south side of the creek and allow time for Price and Shelby to get to Fort

Scott and complete that conquest. First, however, he had to cross the creek. This certainly would be conventional military thinking, but they didn't have the ability to use this plan as the Union cavalry was upon them. Conventional military thinking—and Marmaduke was a West Point graduate—would have dictated that, according to Gott, "a covering force would contain perhaps 1/3rd of your military force, not two thirds which was too heavy for a covering force." He went on to add that, at this point, an effective screening force would call for a "different deployment which would include mobility."

Marmaduke was out of time, however. He needed to do something now. He was fearful, most likely, that he simply could not hold off a concerted Union charge long enough to get the ford cleared, get the remainder of the wagons underway and form a proper defense on the south side of the creek. If Marmaduke was to do anything at all, he was going to have to make a stand here and face the Union cavalry. Marmaduke began preparing his defense. He formed his line, according to Buresh, "perpendicular to the Fort Scott road about 300 yards to the north of the creek. The line extended for about 800 yards with the right resting on the ravine on the right flank and the left formed on a small hillock on the left flank immediately north of the northernmost bend in Mine Creek." This force also decided to fight on horses, which ran counter to the normal doctrines of the Confederate army. Typically, they would move their horses off to the rear and dismount. They would then come back forward to form their battle lines. This decision was to prove costly to the Rebels as the Union cavalry brought its forces to bear.

The Rebels were, for the most part, still armed with muzzleloading rifles, which were difficult to reload on horseback. With Marmaduke's men and Cabell's brigade in position, and Fagan's coming up into the lines, the Rebels were diligently working to form an effective screening force. A map of the battlefield shows that the Confederate positions were, at the time of the Union charge, arrayed in a northwest–southeast line across the front. Marmaduke's division was situated in two separate front lines and straddled the Fort Scott road, with the creek running about three hundred yards behind them. The Third Missouri was inserted behind the gap in Marmaduke's line where the Fort Scott road ran through it. Here the men placed a battery of guns facing right at the Union lines. The Fourth Missouri was pushed out to the division's far right flank and faced to the northeast alongside a gun battery. Cabell's brigade was brought up and placed right behind the left side of Marmaduke's left flank and was linked up with Fagan's division, which took position to Marmaduke's left and stretched out to the northwest. This made for an imposing force and must have looked like quite a daunting task for the

Union troops to overcome. The line stretched about half a mile across the Union front.

These Rebel soldiers were, however, in no real condition to face the Union cavalry. Most were cold, tired, hungry and demoralized by this point in the campaign, having faced these men in blue several times over the last couple of days and having been defeated each time. To compound the problem, their armaments were no real match for the Union troopers. They were firing muzzleloading rifles from the backs of horses, with no real opportunity to reload. The most these men could hope for was to squeeze off one shot before the enemy was upon them. Additionally, they were arrayed in such a way that there was little chance to repulse a strong attack. Benteen and Phillips knew it, too. Benteen stated in his after-action report that "seeing the position in which he had his artillery, I immediately surmised that the Rebel commander had committed a fatal blunder, and resolved to capture it."

Marmaduke had indeed committed a series of such mistakes. He had the manpower and could have initiated the charge against the Federals before they had a chance to set their own line of battle; this may have caused the Union troops to fall back to their main body and bought Marmaduke more time to set a more desirable defense. He also could have worked to get his troopers split behind the creek so that he had a sufficient screening force behind the creek, in which case, according to Gott, "the Unions troops may have ridden up and decided that they wanted nothing to do with that and retreated back, and allowed extra time for Price to get away." This defense, however, was completely committed in a line and had given up its mobility. This was a static defense with a large creek directly to the rear.

The Union troops were situated in front of the Rebels several yards to their front. As stated earlier, the Fort Scott road essentially split Phillips's and Benteen's brigades in two. Phillips, who had arrived at the battlefield a little before Benteen, had chosen to form three different lines, with the First Missouri State Militia situated toward his front, running in a line from northwest to southeast and facing the center of Marmaduke's line. Behind, one hundred yards and slightly to the west, the Seventh Missouri State Militia waited, was situated basically along a north–south line and was facing toward Marmaduke's left, occupied by Freeman and Cabell. Immediately to their right was the Fourth Missouri State Militia facing the same direction, which was directly to the front of the left of Fagan's lines occupied by Colonel Dobbin and Slemmons, along with the Forty-seventh Arkansas and additional artillery support.

Phillips's men also were far better armed than their Confederate counterparts. Many were armed with the Spencer rifle, a lever-action rifle, which was manually fed cartridges into the chamber through a tube mounted under the barrel. This allowed the rider to simply chamber another round with the flick of the wrist. The other men were equipped with pistols, sabers and carbines. Many of the Union troopers often carried more than one pistol. This gave the Federal cavalry a decided advantage in firepower. What that meant, it can be argued, is that the Union troopers could have easily fired a dozen or more shots into the Rebel ranks in the same time it took the enemy to fire off a single shot. Total strength for Phillips's brigade was at about 1,500 well-armed, motivated and fearless men who were fresh off a great victory at Westport in which they played a key role.

Benteen's regiments were lined up in four ranks, one behind the other, on the east side of the Fort Scott road. They did not change their disposition in the least, so that meant for the charge that the regiments would follow one another into the battle. The ranks, which numbered about 1,100 strong, were led again by the Tenth Missouri, followed by the Fourth Iowa and the Third Iowa; the consolidated Seventh Indiana/Fourth Missouri brought up the rear. As was the case with Phillips's men, this was a veteran brigade that was well armed and motivated. Much of the brigade had seen extensive action in the East and had experienced great success. The men had been marching together for some time and formed as professional a unit as there was on the field that day. Benteen had not been in command of this regiment for long. He took command from Colonel Winslow during the action at Westport only two days prior, during the fighting at the Big Blue River. Benteen had previously been in command of the Tenth Missouri and was known to be a steady and capable commander who would not put his men into a bad situation, but he was also a very aggressive officer who would take action if he thought that his men would be able to gain the advantage. He was also a very brave man who led his men from the front and would not ask his men to do something that he was unwilling to do himself. Like a great many of his men, Benteen was fueled by a desire to rid the area of the Rebel threat. Both Phillips and Benteen had ridden the hard road through Missouri and into Kansas and wanted to get rid of the Rebels so they would not have to deal with them anymore.

Another odd dichotomy was at play. Most of the men on both the Union and Confederate sides were from Missouri. Missouri was, obviously, a hotly contested state between the North and the South. Missourians were fighting Missourians on the Kansas side of the state line: "This was to be a fight of brother against brother and neighbor against neighbor, with the Fourth Missouri Cavalry [Union] against the Fourth Missouri Cavalry [Confederate] on the east flank and the Seventh Missouri State Militia [Union] against the

Seventh Missouri Cavalry [Confederate] in the center." With this sort of local hatred for one another, it was plain to see how a Union trooper in Benteen's or Phillips's brigade could muster the courage to make one final charge into what appeared to be an exceedingly difficult situation.

The two brigades also were, by a stroke of good luck, very complementary units. Phillips's brigade, armed with heavier weapons and the ability to fight effectively dismounted, were able to really support Benteen's charge once he began. Benteen's men, a veteran cavalry force, were accustomed to the charge and were prepared to hit the enemy hard in the teeth. In modern terms, you can almost consider a great cavalry charge to consist of "shock and awe." The cavalrymen were the ultimate "shock troops" who could hit an enemy at speed and really knock them off balance. They could break through a line and be behind you in a matter of minutes. Phillips's men, to complement the charge, could lay down an effective base of fire on the defenders with their long range and repeating rifles, the rate of fire of which the Rebels simply could not match. Buresh noted that "[t]his was an excellent combination of the three basic characteristics of cavalry, i.e., fire power, mobility, and shock action."

With this, the battle lines were formed and the two armies were set to face off. As Benteen had alluded to earlier, October 25 was a glorious Kansas day, with a bright sun and cool temperatures. The ground was also perfect for maneuvering cavalry. Marmaduke's men had the advantage of numbers with his force outmanning the Union by more than two to one. He had seemingly made serious errors when placing his men in position to take on the attackers. His back was to the creek, he had no room to maneuver and he had no effective reserve force to fill gaps in the line exploited by the Union forces. On the other side, the Federal cavalry had superior firepower and the ability to hit the Rebels where they could best be effective. They were, however, tired. Both horse and man had been on the march for hundreds of miles for the last several weeks. Additionally, since the fight at Westport, there had been very little to eat for either. The horses were jaded and the men were exhausted. To charge once more into the breach against what appeared to be insurmountable odds was going to require a herculean effort. The men of the two Union brigades would be tested to their limits on this day.

As the action unfolded, Lieutenant Colonel Frederick Benteen surveyed the situation and made a fateful decision. He was under orders to charge at his own discretion. Here was a situation in which the odds were against them, but Benteen decided that there was no time like the present. He had

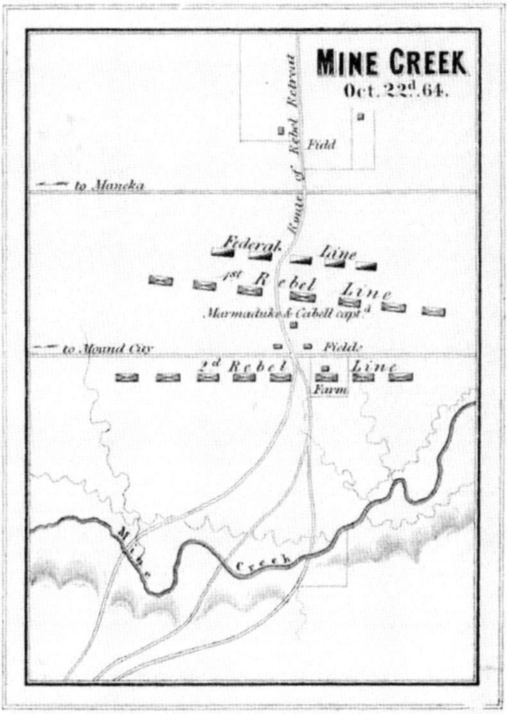

The Battle of Mine Creek. *Courtesy of the Kansas State Historical Society.*

spotted major problems within the Rebel ranks and was prepared to exploit them. He knew that his troops were better armed and more confident as well. He sent word to the brigade on his right, not entirely certain of who was in command, and requested that it charge at the same time so that they could hit both flanks simultaneously. In his own words, "I sent an officer to the commanding officer of the brigade on my right with the information that I was going to charge, and a request for him to charge with me, for God's sake." With those words, the Battle of Mine Creek was underway and was bound for the history books as the greatest battle ever fought on Kansas soil. In fact, it would be the only battle fought in Kansas between uniformed Union and Confederate troops.

Chapter 7

"Boot to Boot, Stirrup to Stirrup"

This attack would not have been possible had Mine Creek been between them.
—Senior Military Historian Kendall Gott, U.S. Army, Fort Leavenworth, Kansas

It is clear that an attack did happen on this day, October 25, 1864. The horses and men, nearly one thousand of them, faced one another across a long stretch of Kansas prairie. The Confederate army, led by Sterling Price, had been on the march across Kansas and had experienced great military success up to the Battle of Westport. At Westport, his Rebel army was defeated completely and sent into the borderlands that separated the states of Kansas and Missouri. Now, Confederate major general John Sappington Marmaduke stood with his back to a creek in eastern Kansas and had nowhere to go. He would have to make a stand if his army had any chance to escape certain destruction at the hands of the Union Army of the Border, which was bent on revenge and wanted the Rebel invaders pushed out of the area and back to the lands of the Confederacy.

The day started out gray but became a sunlit and beautiful fall Kansas day. Lieutenant Colonel Benteen had come across the area just to the north of Mine Creek, in what is Linn County, Kansas, a few miles to the west of Mound City. Colonel Phillips was already in position waiting for reinforcements so that he could combat the large Confederate force. The positions were set—Phillips's brigade on the right and Benteen's on the left. Benteen was sure of the nature of his troops and felt them to be a far

An engraving of a cavalry charge published in *Harper's Weekly. Author's collection.*

superior force to that of the Rebels. After all, they had beaten them already, they were better armed and the Rebels had clearly not set themselves up for success by placing themselves between the Union force and the creek. Unlike Marmaduke, who failed to take the initiative and seize the opportunity to initiate contact with the enemy, Benteen knew that fast action was critical. As Benteen moved into position, he sent word to the brigade commander to his left, still uncertain of who it was, that he was going to charge and that it would be appreciated if he would support them by charging at the same time. "Benteen gave the order: Draw sabers! His own Tenth Missouri Regiment in the lead sounded off with a big yell. He then gave the orders: 'Attention to charge! Forward! March!'"

Benteen's troops moved out. At this point, the horses were spent from the long marches of the previous days. Typically, when the cavalry advances, the horses do not charge off at full gallop at the sound of the bugle as in Hollywood pictures. They begin at a walk and then advance to a trot, finally hitting full gallop as they crash into the wall of enemy facing them. In this case, given that both men and horses were so extremely fatigued, it is probably likely that the horses were only able to trot quickly or perhaps break into a slow gallop into battle, unlike in normal circumstances. Still, they advanced on the Rebel positions as fast as their mounts would take them.

Benteen had taken his rightful position at the front of his brigade and was waving his saber in the air with the rest of his men. The Confederate artillery began to open fire on the advancing blue-coated cavalry dashing toward them. The Rebel troops just waited in silence as the Federals bore down upon them. Benteen could see to his right that Phillips had not begun the charge at the same time as his force but would be slightly behind him when he hit the Rebel forces. Benteen's Federals were headed directly into Marmaduke's guns. Terror filled the eyes of many of the Confederates both young and old. Although many had seen combat during the march through Missouri and into Kansas, most had never faced a cavalry charge and were wholly unprepared for this sort of tactic. At Westport, it was much more a "long gun battle," with limited traditional cavalry charges. Much more

An engraving of cavalry in action, published in the *Illustrated London News. Courtesy of Douglas W. Bostick.*

emphasis was placed on dismounted cavalry and artillery, and the battle was, for the most part, fought at greater distances.

Men on both sides of the lines were tense. Phillips's brigade, for example, was made up of Missouri Militia units that had been fighting against guerillas for the most part. Until Westport, many of them had never lined up opposite the Rebel lines and gone head to head in the type of battle typically seen throughout the Civil War. Benteen's brigade was the exception, though. Many of his troops had fought in several of the major cavalry encounters in the East. With the exception of many of Benteen's men, most of these men had not seen thousands of screaming men brandishing sabers and firing their carbines while mounted atop snorting, galloping horses headed straight for them. As impressive as it must have been for the Union cavalry to stare out at the long line of Rebel soldiers and guns, it must have been an equally, if not more awesome, sight to witness this impressive line of Union men thundering toward them.

Suddenly, all was not right. Surely the Rebels would begin crumbling at the sight of 2,700 men and beasts charging them. This was not the case. The Rebel troopers, sitting bravely in their saddles, stood static in their defensive positions, stiffened and waiting for the first horse to crash into their lines with a determination to stand their ground. The advance ground to a halt. The Tenth Missouri had inexplicably and suddenly halted. The men and horses of the Fourth Iowa, the Third Iowa and the consolidated Seventh Indiana/Fourth Missouri were stacking up behind the Tenth until it became one mass of horse and man turning about and waiting for what was to come, wondering what had happened.

Benteen was livid. This was his very own Tenth Missouri regiment, the regiment that he was commanding when Colonel Winslow fell and he was tasked with taking over. What had happened? Lieutenant Colonel Benteen "rode out in front of his brigade within pistol shot of the enemy." He then yelled and pleaded with his men to continue the charge to the backdrop of the strains of his buglers still sounding the notes of the charge. Slowly the regiments moved forward, but not far. The mess was untangling but there was still no resuming the charge. Time was ticking fast.

Meanwhile, on the right, Phillips saw Benteen's men screech to a halt. He had little choice but to stop as well. Perhaps Benteen saw something he didn't. Phillips did, however, begin the offensive on his own. One of his brigades, the First Missouri State Militia, led by Bazel Lazear, had the foresight to dismount from its horses and begin putting fire to the elements in front of it. Compared to what the Confederates could answer with, its firepower was remarkable. Bullets streaked through Marmaduke's men, who stood directly in front of Lazear's regiment. For the moment, however, the charge had stopped. The momentum was lost, and the Union forces were looking at one another and wondering what to do. Benteen's soldiers were just milling around within rifle shot of the Rebels, staring at them with anger but wholly unwilling to charge at them.

When considering the mistakes made by Marmaduke, Fagan and more, one has to imagine that one of the largest was the fact that, having lost most or all of their mobility, the Rebels were completely unprepared to exploit any mistakes that the Union troops might have made. A charge right at the Union troops very likely would have caused them to withdraw. In this situation, Benteen's men were just sitting in their saddles, and Phillips's men, although at least pouring fire on the enemy, were doing the same thing. Here was the opportunity. Instead, the Rebels stood motionless, still braced for the charge. Perhaps it was fatigue, perhaps it was fear or perhaps it was a little of both. The fact was that the Battle of Mine Creek was becoming a battle that might not happen at all unless someone took the initiative.

This impetus came in the form of Regimental Commander Abail R. Pierce of the Fourth Iowa. Pierce moved to the front of his regiment and began shouting orders. Ordering his men to move their column to the left so that they were clear of the Tenth Missouri in front of them, Pierce prepared to do the unthinkable. He ordered his men into columns and went to the front of the line. He pulled out his saber, waved it in the air and waited for his bugler to sound the charge. Once he did, the Iowans began their charge, rolling right past the stunned Missourians, who could only shout encouraging words to them as they made their thrust toward the enemy. By this time, all of the Fourth Iowa was charging hard toward the Confederates, who had to be as stunned as anyone at the audacity of the Iowans' mad rush. Soon thereafter, the remainder of Benteen's men began to follow. Phillips's brigade also looked on with amazement; his men remounted (those who had dismounted to provide firepower) and began forward again.

The lead elements of Pierce's regiment hit the Rebel right with an unbelievable crash. The Rebel Fourth Missouri Cavalry, Burbridge's men, were shocked to see the Iowans cut through their line in rapid fashion and began to run away as fast as they could in abject panic. Clark's brigade, just to the northwest of Burbridge's cavalry, was the next to feel the brunt of the cavalry charge. Following behind were the other regiments of Benteen's command—all of them crashing into the Confederate troops and hitting them with a great force. Phillips was also not far behind and began slamming into the lines alongside his Union compatriots.

An engraving of Union cavalry in battle, published in the *Illustrated London News. Courtesy of Douglas W. Bostick.*

A sketch of the Battle of Mine Creek, Kansas, by Samuel J. Reader. *Author's collection.*

Another criticism about this battle, often directed at Marmaduke, was his decision to place the untested brigade under Thomas Freeman, which had only been formed just before Price invaded Missouri, directly in the center of the defenses. This brigade began to break and run before they even made direct contact with the Union horsemen. This brigade was not one of Marmaduke's finer regiments, with many of the men described as "unmotivated conscripts while others were former deserters and could not be expected to take the heavy fire in spite of attempts by their officers to hold them firm." This was the very same brigade that, only minutes earlier, had been under intense fire from Lazear's riflemen. Given the heat of battle, with the bullets flying everywhere and men falling dead and wounded all around, it is little wonder that a green brigade like Freeman's would have a tremendous amount of trouble standing and fighting against such a force of arms from the Union troopers.

With the mad scramble by Freeman's brigade to get out of harm's way, the other brigades began to fall like dominoes. Freeman's brigade represented a major force that stood in the way of the Union advance. At this point, many of the men from the right began to crumble when they saw Freeman's troopers make a dash to the rear and joined in. Freeman's brigade was a mess. Everywhere around them was panic. With the disposition of the Rebel lines, there was nowhere to go. The ford had been blocked, and there was a mad scramble to get across the creek. All along the Confederate right, Benteen's men were wreaking havoc on the beleaguered defenders. Units were not withdrawing in good order as they had, for the most part, during the brunt of the campaign—this time it was a mad scramble. Panic ensued along the line as many of the Rebels just wanted to get away from the terror being wrought upon them by the troopers in Benteen's brigade.

Colonel Phillips was having similar success down the line to the Confederate left. His men brought terror down upon the Rebel left, charging with pistols in their hands and firing madly. They hit the Confederates with an incredible power and speed that simply stunned the Rebels—striking them "like a thunderbolt" from over the rise of the hill that shielded their advance until they were very close to the lines. The lines along the front of Phillips's men were falling apart, just as they were on Benteen's side. Phillips's brigade was able to roll into the enemy lines and, with so many defenders running for their lives, turn the flank of Cabell's brigade, ultimately pushing them back toward the rear. All was not lost along the lines, however. Many units continued to fight on bravely in spite of the incredible crush upon their ranks. The brigade of Clark's men was still standing strong despite losing half of its one thousand men, mostly to fleeing. The troops who remained with their commander were pushing back at the Federal units where they could and trying to stand firm at the urging of General Marmaduke. The troops who were continuing to put up a fight were from, "Jeffer's Eighth Missouri Cavalry, the Seventh Missouri Cavalry, and Davies' Battalion under Lieutenant Colonel J.F. Davies, Colonel Robert R. Lawthers Tenth Missouri Cavalry, and Wood's Cavalry Battalion under Lieutenant Robert C. Wood and Marmaduke's bodyguard commanded by Captain D.E. Stallard," according to Buresh. These men fought bravely, but it simply was going nowhere.

The fighting was certainly different from what either army had experienced at any point in the Missouri Campaign. Fighting went on "boot to boot, stirrup to stirrup" in the midday sun. The weight of the overwhelming firepower and the audacity and speed of the charge had taken the Confederates largely out of the fight at this point. Rebels left their horses and weapons on the field and dashed for any cover they could find. A split-rail fence ran north–south on the north side of the bank across from the Palmer house, which was one of the few homes in the immediate area. Men dove for cover at the base of this fence. Many others tried to get away by scaling the banks of the creek on foot and began running to the south hoping to escape. Fighting was still going on in the center of the line, where the aforementioned Rebel units tried in vain to stop the Union men. Swords clanked against the gun barrels of the Rebel rifles, horsed snorted, men shouted and guns fired. Soon, however, the battle was all but decided as the last throes of combat echoed through the area and the loud reports of a Confederate gun that had fallen into the hands of their enemy was trained upon the men who were desperately running to save their lives.

A battery of Rebel guns also continued to fire on in desperation despite the fact that the battle was completely winding down. All along the line, the last skirmishes were waning as the Rebel soldiers increasingly sought to reach the safety of the south side of Mine Creek or the fields beyond. The last of the lines to fall was being eliminated by elements of Benteen's troopers, who ran through the line and reached the creek. Here they set to work trying to block any possible exit that the enemy may try to use to escape. The left side of the Rebel line was the last to fall back simply due to the fact that Phillips's brigade had not joined the charge immediately when Benteen's men did. It instead stayed behind and provided fire support before quickly remounting and joining the charge. The men fought with all of the bravery that they could muster but were finally eliminated. The fighting was still raging, but the die had been cast. The battle was clearly ending, and it would be the

Union men who would carry the day. It is reported that cheers began to be heard all up and down the lines from the victorious Union troops.

Slemmons and Dobbin were among the last of the holdouts of the Rebel forces. They were slowly being pushed back, however, under the weight of the Union charge. At this point, the Federal charge stopped and became a pursuit. Men were cheering along the banks of Mine Creek as the last of the enemy forces was being chased down and captured. Dobbin's and Slemmons's brigades were slowly being pushed back and were finding little in the way of escape routes. Having been trapped against the creek, Colonel Slemmons was finally captured. The remainders of Dobbin's men finally were able to find their way to an area of the creek that had few troops around and made their way toward the relative safety of the opposite bank. Slemmons, having been captured, was one of the first great prizes of the day. Generals Curtis and Pleasonton were finally making their way toward the front as the final minutes of the battle came to a close, and they were able to watch as the last of the Confederates were finished off by the Union troops.

Union general Alfred Pleasonton.
Author's collection.

Countless Rebel troops who had just been pounded by the Federals were now trying everything in their power to escape capture. Hundreds of them simply threw their arms down and left by whatever means they could. Many had lost their horses, and those who were still astride their mounts were fighting hard to just get across the rain-swollen creek with its slippery banks. This caused incredible confusion as men and horses attempted to flee the onslaught of Union soldiers. Many of the Confederate troopers who were desperately seeking a way to get across Mine Creek to the relative safety of the south side were simply not able to make it across because of the condition of the soggy mire along the creek bed and the steep cliffs that hung over it. Men were drowned by the weight of their own horses that had fallen on top of them in the scramble, and men on foot were crushed under the weight of the riotous masses fleeing for their lives.

Federal troopers continued to fire on the refugees and hack at them with their swords, exacting revenge and frustration as they rode them down. As they fled, they passed the dead and dying as they lay prostrate along the ground, surrounded by dead and dying horses, discarded rifles, equipment and ammunition either dropped by the dead and wounded or discarded by the men trying to make their hasty retreat. In short, it was a scene of utter destruction for the Confederates. Men were running all around. Some still attached to small bits of their units were desperately trying to cross the creek and rejoin the army, and many just turned and fled alone in front of the Union enemy.

The Battle of Mine Creek only lasted about fifteen or twenty minutes, but it had taken an awful toll on Marmaduke's and Fagan's men. The weight of seven thousand Southerners had been unable to stand up to the incredible display of bravery and nearly flawless tactical prowess exhibited by Benteen's and Phillips's men, who were better armed, better trained and more motivated. They were spurred by the desire to hit the Rebels and push them out of Kansas so that they wouldn't have to deal with them anymore. Many of them certainly had revenge on their minds as well. They had witnessed the atrocities that the Army of Missouri was capable of only the night before at Trading Post and Marais des Cygnes. By "chance alignment" and no interference from their commanders, these two brigades had performed an amazing feat of arms. It was literally a textbook military maneuver that would make a modern armored cavalry commander swell with pride. They completely shocked their enemy and sent them scrambling in disarray in a short time.

Was it the audacity of Benteen and Phillips that carried the day? They really didn't have a great idea as to whom they were facing because, according to Gott, it was difficult to "look into field glasses and see how the Rebels were armed. Did they know that these were mounted infantry armed with muskets? Not knowing their enemy's armaments made it that much more of an audacious charge." This can be argued because of the fact that neither side really knew the other that well. Gott went on to say, "Unlike units in the East where brigades faced one another many times, they really didn't know who they were fighting. The Fourth Iowa had been fighting guerillas; they didn't know the Fifteenth Arkansas."

Conversely, it must also be noted that Rebel errors contributed massively to the crushing defeat. Marmaduke made several serious mistakes in the displacement of his forces. With a creek so close behind him, it was nearly impossible to be able to maneuver his troops effectively. Much blame must also be placed at the feet of Marmaduke and Fagan for troop alignment. For example: Freeman's brigade was placed in the center of the line. This proved to be extremely costly, as most of the unit broke and ran even before the Federals had gotten to within range. They simply ran. To be an effective screening force, Gott said, "You must put something between you and your enemy: in the case, the creek." The mindset of the Rebel rear guard must also be taken into account. The decision was made; they just wanted to get to the safety of Arkansas. They wanted nothing more to do with the Union army. This was a sentiment felt not only by the commanders but also by the rank and file. In short, this was a complete disaster for Price's army that had as much to do with the bravery of the attackers as it did with the mistakes made by the Confederates. In a letter to Major General Curtis, Major A.R. Pierce, commanding the Fourth Iowa Veteran Cavalry, wrote:

> *General: Fearing that justice will not be done my regiment in the battle of Osage, I take the liberty to call your attention to the charge made by them on the enemy's right, at a time when our line on the right had halted and were receiving a destructive fire from the enemy. At that time a perfect rout of our line appeared to be almost certain. My regiment had just formed on the extreme left of our line when I commenced the charge. The three companies on the right of my regiment charged through the line of the Tenth Missouri Volunteer Cavalry Regiment, which was formed in their front. In that charge we crushed the enemy's right completely. We cut them so close that I cut eight Rebels from their horses with my own saber. My regiment captured over 200 prisoners with two stand of colors. We advanced so far into the enemy's ranks that Major-General Pleasonton ordered our own battery to shell us, thinking we were the retreating enemy, and my men were*

Confederate general John Sappington Marmaduke. *Courtesy of the Missouri State Historical Society.*

> *obliged to scatter to avoid being cut to pieces by our own shells. I should have called to see you, general, had not I received a severe wound in my foot, which prevents my riding my horse.*

General Marmaduke did stick by his men to the last. He had continued to try to turn his troops around and rally them to victory. Many of his most trusted troops stuck by his side as he tried in vain to stem the tide of the Union advance and buy additional time for Price to put additional distance between him and Curtis's army. This dedication to duty resulted in another of the great prizes of the day. Private James Dunlavy of the Third Iowa Cavalry was the man to deliver a great blow to Price. Marmaduke had been attempting to re-form a small unit composed of men who had become separated from their units; Dunlavy rode up on Marmaduke, firing as he went. At first, the general thought that it was another of the Rebel stragglers and was yelling at him to hold his fire. As he approached, Dunlavy realized who sat on the horse in front of him: a Confederate general. Dunlavy ordered Marmaduke off his horse while still leveling his gun at him. Dunlavy had bagged a great prize. He marched the general back toward the rear of the battlefield, where he came upon one of General Curtis's men, Colonel Blair. Colonel Blair was suitably impressed by this prisoner and shortly delivered him to General Curtis at the home of W.H. Ragains, which was nearby just off of the Mound City Road. General Pleasonton then arrived at Marmaduke's request. He was concerned that he was "being taken captive by vengeful Kansas troops." The two men met and talked for quite a while. Marmaduke was now a prisoner of war. Private Dunlavy would later be awarded a Congressional Medal of Honor for his capture of Marmaduke.

General Cabell was also an unfortunate captive of the Union army after he and a group of about twenty men tried to run for it. They attempted to run through a detachment of Union troopers that was stationed along the

Confederate general William L. Cabell. *Courtesy of the Missouri State Historical Society.*

creek looking for stragglers who might have wished to run. They managed to elude their would-be captors, but not for long. Cabell was taken by the men and sent to the rear. They were unaware of the man's identity because he had concealed his rank by covering it with his coat and buttoning it up completely. As he made his way back toward the Union lines, he ran across a horse that was wandering alone on the battlefield. Again he made a break for it, and again he was captured. This new set of troopers sent him back toward the rear to be rounded up by the prison detail. Being the wily commander he was, he ran across another horse and attempted another escape. This time he was nabbed by the same group that had found him just minutes before, a unit under the command of Sergeant Calvary Young of the Third Iowa Cavalry. Cabell was desperate to escape because he was a wanted man. The Union soldiers who had faced him before despised him. He was unfortunately forced to identify himself and was quickly moved to the rear by Young in case any Union soldiers decided to exact revenge on the general. Sergeant Young would also later be awarded a Congressional Medal of Honor for bringing in General Cabell. This brought the total of captured high-ranking field commanders to three: General Marmaduke, General Cabell and Colonel Slemmons. Many other high-ranking officers were captured during the action at Mine Creek, including two generals, three full colonels and many lieutenant colonels and majors.

As mentioned earlier, the successful raid on Glasgow, Missouri, only days before had netted the Rebels, along with rifles and ammunition, a great number of Union overcoats. The fall weather in Kansas had begun to render it quite cold, especially at night. The Confederates distributed the overcoats among the men after they secured them in Glasgow, and the men gladly accepted them because of the temperature. This was to prove costly for many of the men taken prisoner that day, as a great many were executed on the spot for wearing them. It was standard procedure in Missouri that men captured wearing Union uniforms be killed. Most often this applied to guerillas, but in this case, many remembering their own men taken prisoner and being executed took the order to its letter and killed many other men outright. There were simply too many instances of Confederate guerillas or regular units killing Union men to be ignored. Just a year earlier, Lawrence had also been raided and burned by Quantrill, after all. About two hundred mostly unarmed men and boys were killed in cold blood.

Numbers of killed and wounded for the day were fairly high, despite the short duration of the battle, with numbers of dead anywhere between two hundred and four hundred being killed and about two hundred being wounded; about five hundred prisoners were taken. Given the higher number of dead compared to wounded, it is likely that the execution of prisoners certainly played a large part in this. Union casualties were, conversely, extremely light for a battle of this size. The Union listed eight men killed and about sixty wounded. Also among the spoils for the Army of the Border were a huge amount of horses, arms and ammunition, eight cannons that the Rebels had to abandon and a large number of wagons. All of this was gathered up and much of it placed up at the Ragains home, where General Curtis was currently located. Curtis appointed a man, Lieutenant Colonel John Sears, to take command of the secured area and deal with the prisoners and captured equipment.

The Battle of Mine Creek was over. It was as complete a victory as could be expected of an inferior force attacking a force with overwhelming numerical superiority. Many Rebels were, however, still on the loose in Kansas and were headed straight south toward Fort Scott and the military stores there. Curtis's Army of the Border still had a job to do. One can surmise that, although this was a great and crushing victory for the Federals, the Rebels were also able to take something away from it. A great percentage of the army was still intact, including Shelby's entire division, and Price's army still posed a threat to the free state. Arnold Schofield, administrator for the Mine Creek Battlefield State Historic Site at Pleasanton, Kansas, said, "Not only was the Battle of Mine Creek a Union victory—as was everything after Westport—but it was also the execution of a successful Confederate rear-guard action."

Chapter 8

The Confederates Break and Run

The Battle of Mine Creek was over. The Confederate divisions of Fagan and Marmaduke had been smashed and sent running in front of the hooves of the Union cavalry. They now had to attempt to regroup and figure out a way to get back to Price's main body, all the while continuing to perform their duty to provide a successful rear guard action and prevent the Northerners from catching the wagons and crushing the remainder of the Army of Missouri. Men were streaming south as fast as their horses or feet could carry them. Benteen and Phillips, the heroes of Mine Creek, were soon to take up their pursuit along with the rest of the army.

As the mounted Federals began their pursuit, they could see the remnants of the Rebel army moving in disarray toward the south. Benteen and Phillips would again be in the lead of the army. General Fagan ordered a delaying action just south of Mine Creek. One regiment would form a skirmish line as soon as the remnants of the trampled army had passed, but the Union army was clearly too much for this meager force, and the men quickly withdrew south for fear of being overtaken. Benteen and Phillips continued south for about one mile until they ran into yet another line of men showing arms. The Fourth Iowa, which had just finished a monumental charge at Mine Creek, now had another line to take care of. The men got off their mounts and began pushing the skirmishers down the road. Phillips, meanwhile, had run across another line of Fagan's men, which Phillips decided to attack. This small group thought better of it and rapidly left the scene.

At this point, General Pleasonton had ordered Phillips's and Benteen's brigades to stop at once and wait for the main body of the army to arrive before they could continue the pursuit. This could be construed as gross mismanagement of the available troops by Pleasonton given the fact that the additional troops from Sanborn's brigade could have greatly aided in rendering an even greater blow to the Rebels by checking their retreat, capturing more prisoners and perhaps destroying the greater share of Fagan's and Marmaduke's two divisions. Other brigades in Pleasonton's division were stretched back even farther. In all, Curtis's army was stretched from just south of Mine Creek all the way north to Marais des Cygnes, where Blunt, still stinging from Curtis's placement of Pleasonton's division ahead of his, remained. This was a distance of nearly eight miles. It would certainly take a great amount of time to form Blunt's division and move it that many miles south to link up with Pleasonton. Blunt was adamant that his forces had become stalled because of the clog of men, horses and wagons that apparently had not allowed the Marais des Cygnes to be crossed. Most would claim, however, that his unwillingness to move to the aid of the attack was still due to his ego.

Price was many miles away by this time. He was encamped on the Little Osage River, which lay about eight miles to the south of Mine Creek. He

An engraving of a Confederate retreat. *Author's collection.*

received a message while there directly from General Marmaduke regarding the situation at Mine Creek and that he was about to come under attack. At this point, he had to abandon his plan to take Fort Scott. This was a prize that Price desperately needed. There was reported to be a great amount of military supplies there, and this would add to his wagon train of plunder to take back to Rebel territory. His hope was still that his expedition would be viewed as successful if he could bring back as much bounty as he could haul regardless of the fact that his other objectives—the raiding of St. Louis, the taking of Jefferson City and the installing of Governor Reynolds as the Confederate governor—had failed to be met. He ordered Shelby back in the direction of Mine Creek "with whatever troops he could gather together" to help extract Marmaduke from the dangerous situation. He hadn't gotten very far when he met the sad mob of men that remained of Cabell's and Marmaduke's shattered divisions. They were running in total disarray from the sight of the horrendous battle.

Despite his best efforts, he could not get the beleaguered Rebel survivors of Mine Creek to stop and re-form. They simply ignored his pleas and continued south. Price was despondent. He had lost General Marmaduke to the Union army and had seen his rear guard crushed and running in fear from its advance. Here was tangible evidence of the massive amount of mistakes that had been made during the campaign. His huge, slow-moving wagon train had caused him to lose sight of the larger picture, and his army was now in disarray. He was now faced with losing the ability to take Fort Scott as well. It would have, most likely, been an easy target for Shelby, and they could have stripped it bare. This desire to carry the albatross of a wagon train around his neck had now likely finished his campaign and doomed it to defeat and humiliation.

Unbeknownst to him, the Army of the Border was still handing him another favor, though. It was mired in its own indecision and lack of quick action due to politics and pride. Blunt was in no way eager to move south to join Pleasonton so they could hasten the attack. He was brooding about having to take up the rear and wanted nothing to do with aiding in allowing Pleasonton to capture more battlefield glory. Meanwhile, they could see the Rebels in the distance continuing toward Fort Scott, with only Colonel Moonlight's force standing in the way. Moonlight was staring at a force led by Brigadier General M. Jeff. Thompson that had been detached to push him back from Price's flanks.

The frightened Rebels continued to stream southward. Shelby now began to set up a defense at the Little Osage River, which was about south of Mine

Creek. Unlike Mine Creek, it is a low river with very little bank at all. It sits in a low-lying area that is very marshy and has a fair amount of trees and brush around it. Thompson's regiments began to move back into the area, and Shelby began to insert them into a line of battle. As at Mine Creek, he kept all of his men on their horses and waited for the Union troopers to appear. Spread out in three ranks, Thompson's men had fine positions and could easily see them coming their way. Pleasonton's men, by this time, had recovered from the action at Mine Creek and were slowly getting themselves organized to continue the pursuit. Just as the Rebels could see the Federals, the reverse was also true. The Northerners began organizing themselves in line of battle.

The Second Kansas Cavalry had reached the forward element by this time and was put in the line alongside the brigades of Phillips and Sanborn, who had also been brought forward. Benteen had, by this time, halted his brigade. The Union force facing Thompson's brigade was about three thousand strong, which was considerably smaller than what it had started with at Mine Creek. The men formed into line and began their advance toward Thompson. Thompson was able to muster about two thousand men. By this time, Benteen had already begun to get his brigade back into their saddles and move out as well. Farther away from this action, General Blunt and his men were still attempting to move south but were moving slowly toward the Union forces. They would obviously take a great deal of time to catch up to Pleasonton's division. As they moved forward, they were plainly able to see all of the debris that had been left behind by the panicked Rebels who had fled through the area just before.

McNeil, Sanborn and Phillips continued their advance rapidly, and at about 2:00 p.m., the Rebel pickets placed along a wooded area just north of the Little Osage River were rousted from their positions and began to fall back. There was to be no action because, as had happened several times before, the skirmishers were not eager to take on the Union troopers and fled without firing a shot. At this point, General Pleasonton was anxious to get moving and ordered a charge on the Confederate positions. The Union men charged hard. One of the units, the Fifth Missouri State Militia, was asked to make a charge and eliminate a wooden fence that stood in the way of the advance. The Fifth Missouri made the charge and got the fence taken down despite taking a great amount of fire from the Rebel lines. Men were charging hard at the Rebel positions. Many wanted to get into the action for the first time and get their share of the glory. Buresh noted that "[s]ome regiments charged with sabers in the air while others made the charge with pistols blazing. The bugles blew, and with great cheer, they thundered forward."

The Union troops swept toward the Confederate positions with vigor. Thompson's men held their ground until the enemy was near, and then he opened fire with a volley from his front rank and then beat a hasty retreat to the rear. Thompson's men rushed to the south in much the same manner as Marmaduke's and Fagan's men did at Mine Creek. Thompson's officers were eventually able to get the frightened Rebels calmed and back into formation. The first two lines had fallen back rapidly, but the third was in an excellent defensive position and began to fire on the rushing Federals. After a spirited defense, the third line was eventually pushed back and reformed. At this time, Benteen and Phillips had begun making their way to support McNeil. Thompson's men continued to make lines, allow the Federals to advance, fire a volley and then retreat, hastily burning, just as at Westport, anything that they could light to cover them along the way. Shelby had been part of the action throughout but had continued to fall back in desperation.

The Rebels would form line after line to cover the wagons by impeding the Union advance. This went on for about an hour before Thompson was forced to break off his covering action and make his way rapidly toward the wagon train, which was still slowly beating its retreat toward Arkansas. This action was made by extremely tired men who were riding on jaded horses and unable to cover much ground. Again, however, the Rebels had done what they were tasked with doing: they slowed the Union advance to a crawl. The "Battle of the Little Osage" was little more than a delaying action that succeeded in allowing precious time for Price to make his way southward and ever closer to Confederate territory. Casualties reported for each side were very light. Given that everyone was moving so slowly, there was little chance of making too much headway against the Rebel defenders.

Price was still holding on to his wagons and trying desperately to get across the state line into Arkansas. He had, by this time, decided that he had no time or ability to attack Fort Scott, so he turned toward the southeast instead of keeping his route to Fort Scott. By this point, it had become a race against time. Would he be able to keep what was left of his army intact and get his wagons into Rebel territory? He was sure going to try. Ultimately, Price reached the edge of the Marmiton River at a point just east of Fort Scott. He was going to have to effect a crossing with his huge wagon train and would have to organize a defense for it. It is telling of the man's tenacity that, after the massive defeat at Mine Creek, he was still willing to put his troops at risk and cover a retreat instead of divesting himself of this massive detriment to his progress.

Confederate general Joseph O. Shelby. *Courtesy of the Missouri State Historical Society.*

Shelby once again would need to cover his retreat by organizing a covering force that would buy Price enough time to get his wagons across the steep-banked river. Not falling into the same trap that Marmaduke had, Shelby placed his forces about two miles away in the direction of the attackers. He also placed his men in force, bringing to bear about eight thousand men both armed and unarmed. By placing the unarmed men in the line of battle—which actually outnumbered the armed men—Shelby hoped that it would look like an impressive force and fool Union commanders into thinking that a direct charge on open ground would be a dangerous proposition.

At about 3:30 p.m., McNeil's men reached Shelby's large force. He assembled his brigade into a line of battle and faced the wall of Confederates. Shelby then ordered the first charge, as McNeil was moving slowly. McNeil's troopers easily repulsed this charge due to the fact that nearly all of the men were unarmed. These Rebels got pounded hard by McNeil's rifles and were forced to withdraw quickly, as many of them were either killed or wounded. At the same time, Benteen pulled his brigade into the line directly to the right of McNeil and took his position, soon to be joined by two sections of artillery. Shelby was in an excellent position to make a charge against the

Union troops but continued to demur. On two separate occasions, McNeil braced for a charge but was unable to get the horses to move, as they were completely spent. Even Major Pierce of the Fourth Iowa, one of the heroes of Mine Creek, was unable to get his horses underway. None of the troops really ever got very close to one another, with the exception of Tyler's unarmed brigade, which did muster a charge but was chewed up by Union rifle fire.

One Rebel charge was made by Colonel Jackman's brigade. It was able to hit the right of the Union line and cause some casualties in the Fourth Iowa, including wounding Major Pierce. The forces were spent. There was simply nothing left in man or beast that could make an impact on the battlefield this day. The setting sun brought about a close to the day's battles. Casualties on both sides of the Battle of the Marmiton River had been light in comparison, but the Rebels did lose about twenty-five men killed and fifty wounded. The Battle of the Marmiton ended quietly as both forces, too fatigued to make a stand at this point, simply faded into the setting sun. They had been marching for days now. Twenty-four hours before the action on the Marmiton, the Rebel army was still an effective fighting force that was well armed and able to hold its own against the Union troops. That night, the Rebel army limped into the night, shattered.

Throughout the night, the Confederates continued to try to get their wagons across the creek. This wagon train had been the curse of the Rebel army since it departed for Missouri, and it continued to be so. A group of "volunteers" was rounded up to aid in pushing the wagons up the steep cliffs of the Marmiton River, which the men finally were able to do at about midnight. The day was finally over. The Army of Missouri had experienced a hellish day beginning at Trading Post and ending at the banks of the Marmiton River. In between, the men had seen delays, rear guard actions and the absolute crushing at Mine Creek. It was at this point that General Price made a decision to divest himself and his men of the huge burden that they had been carrying for so many miles. He ordered the wagons to be burned, as well as most of what lay inside of them. The men could only look on with incredulity. They had risked life and limb to see to it that this giant train of bounty made it to the safety of Confederate territory, and now they could only watch as it burned and became a flaming reminder of the lost hope of the Missouri Campaign.

On the Union side, General Pleasonton was moving toward Fort Scott. He had received word that there were plenty of rations for his hungry men and foraging for his exhausted horses. This made Curtis furious. He was going in the opposite direction of the Rebel troops! They were retiring to the southeast, and he was headed seven miles west. Curtis pled with him to camp where he was so that they could start off early in pursuit of Price and completely finish him. Pleasonton refused and started off anyway. He said simply that his men and horses were in dire need of food and water and that it was to be found in Fort Scott. In fact, he was tired himself. He was in no mood to continue chasing Price south. His main objective was to get back to St. Louis, and he would take any chance he could to get there. Blunt also finally made it to the area and watched as Pleasonton's column moved off to the west toward Fort Scott. Blunt decided that he would do the same, so he took off after Pleasonton. This time, Curtis just watched him go. The only units that remained at the battlefield were McNeil's and Benteen's. They camped there that night without water or food for either man or horse. They simply collapsed where they were standing and went to sleep.

Price continued on early the next morning at about 2:00 a.m., with a hollow shell of the army that had marched triumphantly into Missouri one month before. They had set fire to the wagons, which lit up the night sky with flames and exploding ammunition. Now in Missouri, they continued on through the night toward Carthage. Overnight, they were able to finally make good time and covered well over fifty miles until they arrived in Carthage. Here they were able to feed the men and horses and rest for a bit, but they didn't stay long because they were still concerned that the Union forces could be right behind them. They then headed south and eventually reached the town of Newtonia, where Price felt that he was safe. He decided to remain there for a few days and rest his troops.

The Union troops on the night of the twenty-fifth were, with the exception of McNeil and Benteen, all in Fort Scott. There they were able to find food for themselves and forage for their horses. Here the Union troops stayed until midday on the twenty-sixth. Blunt's force departed at about noon and headed to Missouri, followed by McNeil's men, who had camped at the battlefield on the banks of the Marmiton. They marched on in search of Price. Benteen's brigade, which had stayed the night of the twenty-fifth on the battle field, arrived in Fort Scott on the morning of the twenty-sixth and spent the night there. Blunt's force was greatly diminished after the action of the twenty-fifth, and he had no more than a force of about five thousand men at his disposal to continue the chase. Pleasonton remained in Fort Scott but did send his brigades out in the chase for Price with the exception of Phillips's, which was retained in Fort Scott to guard prisoners and secure all of the supplies and equipment captured from the Confederate army.

Price was in camp at Newtonia and was enjoying the rest that he had been afforded since arriving. Suddenly, he looked out and saw what he most dreaded: Blunt's Federal troops bearing down on them in Newtonia. Blunt took little time in readying his men for battle. He deployed his men in a line, brought up four artillery pieces and was able to put effective fire on the Rebels. Shelby and what was left of Cabell's brigade rushed to meet Blunt. Shelby was able to put a great many more men on the field than could Blunt at this stage since Blunt only had one full brigade, Ford's, and part of another, Jennison's, to face Shelby. Blunt took the initiative to go toward Shelby and had some success simply because of the superior firepower that he possessed. Shelby ultimately was able to get the advantage because, with superior numbers, he could outflank Blunt. Blunt was then forced to draw his forces back. In time, Sanborn's brigade made it to the front and helped

Union general James G. Blunt. *Courtesy of the Kansas State Historical Society.*

An engraving of southwestern Missouri. *Author's collection.*

to turn the tide of the battle by hitting the Rebel flankers off to Blunt's left. The sun began to go down, and the battle was largely over by this point. This long battle was the last of the Missouri Campaign. Many casualties had been seen on both sides of the lines, but it was over.

Blunt's pursuit of Price continued, however. He was eager to catch him and totally destroy his army. On the twenty-ninth, he began to pursue him again but was stopped cold by a telegram from General Rosecrans that stated that all Missouri troops were to halt the pursuit and return to their respective bases. This order deprived him of all four of the brigades that Pleasonton had detached to him, leaving him with an effective force of only about 2,500 men. This was an obvious blow to Curtis, who immediately made for Newtonia and cabled General Ulysses Grant, appealing to him to have the Missouri brigades returned to his command. Grant complied with his request, and word was sent out that these brigades needed to return to Curtis at once. These brigade commanders, however, were not keen to rejoin Curtis in his chase. Benteen was the only one to comply when he arrived back at Curtis's encampment on November 1. McNeil appealed to Rosecrans to be allowed to go back to his home base, which was granted. Phillips was too far along on his march and did not make the journey. Sanborn would not rejoin either. All of the brigade commanders claimed that their men and horses were far too tired to rejoin Curtis. Three of the four did not make it. Benteen, however, did eventually make it back

Union general William S. Rosecrans. *Courtesy of the Kansas State Historical Society.*

to Curtis, whose force was now 3,500 strong because of the addition of Benteen's brigade, and they left in pursuit.

Curtis continued to tail Price all the way through Indian Territory but never did catch him. Price himself had a tough trek through Indian Territory, losing men by the hundreds until he had little of his original force left. Price had no command. His men were all scattered throughout the area, most returning home, never to return. The expedition was a failure despite his claims to the contrary.

Chapter 9

The Aftereffects

The Missouri Campaign was over. In just over a month, Major General Sterling Price had raced gloriously north out of Arkansas and through Missouri in the hopes of securing a great victory for the Confederacy. His aims were clear, and him mission was, in the eyes of the Southerners, noble. It has been made abundantly clear that Price utterly failed. His first goal was to take St. Louis and the rich stores there. Owing to his lack of speed, due in large part to his slow-moving wagons, as well as his desire to destroy General Ewing at Pilot Knob, he was simply unable to get this done. By the time he had turned west, St. Louis had been heavily garrisoned with men and heavy guns and stood as a gleaming Northern-controlled harbinger of events to come.

Leaving this behind, he still had hoped to take his political heavyweight passenger, Governor Thomas C. Reynolds, to Jefferson City and capture that prize and then install Reynolds in the governor's office. When they arrived there, they found it too heavily defended and had to abandon it as well. Without the larger siege guns he would have required to take the city, as well as the fact that he was now being pursued by General Pleasonton's cavalry, he had to make a hasty move toward staunch Rebel territory in Boonville. At this point, however, the Missouri Campaign became less of a "campaign" and more of a "raid." In Boonville, he was able to take a respite from the negativity of the campaign up to that point. For the first time—and last time, as it would turn out—he was treated as the conquering hero that he believed himself to be. Price firmly believed this, too. He was a Missourian through and through. Although he was Virginia-born, he loved his home state of Missouri. He was a former Missouri governor and wanted desperately to deliver it to the Confederacy as a present from him. He despised President Abraham Lincoln and wanted nothing more than to give him a bitter pill to swallow by allowing Missouri to secede to the South and take its rightful place among the proud Confederate State of America.

Boonville gave Price a sense that he was on the right path and that the rest of the state should, and eventually would, welcome his army as liberators rather than occupiers. In Boonville, his men were well fed, his horses were rested and he was able to restock with additional supplies and precious manpower. He was, at this point of the expedition, being chased by an excellent force of cavalry led by Pleasonton. Price was now faced with a choice: he could head back south to Confederate territory in Arkansas or head west toward Kansas City and Leavenworth to capture the huge amount of military stores that supposedly existed at that Union depot in the beating heart of hated Kansas. Since he had to abandon the first two critical goals of his campaign, he was left with, in his mind, little choice but to head for Kansas.

At first, it looked as though it would be a fairly easy trek. He departed Boonville and began kicking the small force of Union troops all the way west. He was able to take Glasgow and obliterate the Union garrison there, gaining more supplies for his men, as well as additional bounty for his ever-burgeoning wagon train. He moved ever closer to Kansas City and was met with stiffer resistance every step of the way. The forces of Major General Curtis's Army of the Border were waiting for him. The Kansas Militia was called to arms, and Major General Pleasonton was hot on his trail. Price was now pinched between two forces. He needed a victory in Kansas City to eliminate the threat to his army and allow him to raid and plunder hated Kansas for all he could. Fate intervened, however, and he was dealt a crushing blow from which he would not recover.

The Battle of Westport signified the beginning of the end for the Army of Missouri. Price suddenly went from being the hunter to the hunted. He turned his wagons south. Due to a gallant stand by his most capable and aggressive leader, General Jo Shelby, as well as slow action on the part of the Union commanders, he was allowed to escape. He headed south as fast as his giant wagon train would let him, plodding along with ox-drawn wagons and marauding bands of his own troops pillaging the land for all they could along the Kansas/Missouri borderlands. He posted a rear guard that was able to keep the Federal troops at bay for most of the journey. He kept moving, unwilling to let go of his one tangible asset from the entire campaign. He was bound for Fort Scott—one more stop along the way that could add to the résumé of the campaign if it could just be taken. Mine Creek became the one final obstacle that he simply could not climb.

Audacity, bravery, foolhardiness and ineptitude—whatever the reasons, this was the crushing end of the Missouri Campaign. It was on the wind-swept prairie in eastern Kansas where Sterling Price's dream of a glorious campaign became a nightmare. Only a few more hours were needed to hold Curtis's Federals at bay. Price could then perhaps have Fort Scott. Because of the failure at Westport, he was unable to claim Leavenworth. He needed Fort Scott. Lieutenant Colonel Frederick Benteen and Colonel John Phillips saw it differently. They were worn, weary and hungry and wanted to rid the North of Price and his men for good. Through the gallant actions of them and their men, they were able to mount a brilliant charge that would go down in history. Outnumbered nearly three to one, they stared down the Confederate force and chose to tempt fate and charge. Heroes emerged, Major Abail Pierce of the Fourth Iowa among the many. Pierce saw his force's charge grind to a halt, and with quick, decisive action, he took the lead and undoubtedly saved the day for the Union forces, who could easily have turned tail and ran or, worse yet, been swallowed whole by a superior Rebel force if they had acted. This was the day, however, that saw how a motivated, well-armed and brave force could turn the tables on a fearful and bedraggled group and claim the glory on the field of battle.

"Old Rebel Price," after the Battle of Mine Creek, continued to run to the safety of the South, never to return with an army. He instead limped back with absolutely nothing to show for his foray except the knowledge that his Missouri Campaign would go down in the history books as one of the most colossal failures of the entire Civil War.

Can the Battle of Mine Creek be considered a "great battle"? Certainly, when compared to the large battles in the East such as Gettysburg, Chancellorsville or Bull Run, it pales in comparison from a standpoint of sheer magnitude. It was simply not that large. There were too few combatants to really make a fair comparison. If it is looked at for what it was and its overall effect on the history of the area and the history of the Civil War as a whole, it can definitely stand on its own merits. The Battle of Mine Creek saw the Missouri Campaign completely fall apart. Had Benteen and Phillips not run across Marmaduke's and Fagan's forces and routed them, Sterling Price would then still have had his army intact, he still would have been in position to take Fort Scott and he would have marched back to Arkansas with a giant wagon load of plunder. His army would have lived to fight another day. They could have easily refitted and come back at another time to raid Kansas and wreak more havoc. The Trans-Mississippi would have been bolstered by this influx of additional troops and would have perhaps been able to hold out longer before surrendering completely. Additional raids launched out of Arkansas or Texas could have been mounted on Union troops, and they could have made it very difficult for supply movements. Certainly the troops who were held in the Trans-Mississippi could not have been released to fight in the East and hasten the end of the war there. After Westport, Price's army was still intact and could put up an effective fight at any time. After Mine Creek, there was no will to fight. Sterling Price's command was gone. There was nothing left. The rising star in Price's ranks, General Jo Shelby, could have gone elsewhere to fight and helped lead other Rebel forces to victory.

Benteen and Phillips made such a great impact on the day as well. Their coordinated charges on the Rebel ranks were studied by commanders everywhere as a perfect example of how to have a mutually supported charge utilizing base of fire to support the charge. This type of tactic is still studied today and is taught to all future commanders in the armored corps.

Another of Price's main goals was to damage the reelection of President Lincoln. A great victory in the Trans-Mississippi could have seriously hurt Lincoln by making it appear that the war was far from over and that Missouri was in danger of slipping away to the Confederacy. Senator Lane, who accompanied the Army of the Border, was also reelected. Had the Rebels not been defeated at Mine Creek, then he and Colonel Samuel Crawford, who won the election against Governor Carney, might not have won their bids.

The Battle of Mine Creek was a battle that had such an impact both militarily and politically in both the Kansas/Missouri area and on the national stage that it would be difficult to not see it as a "great battle."

The battle was over. Price's army was destroyed, the remnants having limped back into Arkansas utterly and totally defeated. Mine Creek truly was the crushing end of the Missouri Campaign.

Chapter 10

Lieutenant Colonel Frederick Benteen's After-Action Report

After-action reports are not generally the most riveting reading material available. A great percentage of them can be mind-numbingly dull, with simple facts, troop movements and dispositions and numbers of killed and wounded. I read Lieutenant Colonel Benteen's report on my first day of research at Watson Library at the University of Kansas and was immediately taken with its eloquence and the ability that it had to really convey a sense of what a battlefield commander saw and heard and what caused him to make the decisions that he would during a given battle. This was actually the first and easiest chapter of this book that I wrote. I certainly hope that you are as captivated and mesmerized as I was when I read this report. It simply does not get more compelling than a first-person actual account of Benteen's own experience from Westport to Fort Scott. This is taken directly from *The War of the Rebellion: Official Records of the Union and Confederate Armies*, series I, volume 41.

Report of Lieut. Col. Frederick W. Benteen, Tenth Missouri Cavalry, commanding Fourth Brigade, Cavalry Division.

Headquarters Fourth Brigade, Cavalry Division, Cross Timbers, MO., November 3, 1864.

General: I beg respectfully to submit the following report of the operations of this brigade since I have had the honor of commanding it:

On the morning of the 23rd of October, Colonel Winslow, commanding, was unfortunately wounded in the leg and had to retire from the field, and the command devolved upon me as the next ranking officer. At the time I felt the enemy well posted on the opposite side of the Big Blue with a very strong position and in considerable numbers. Captain Dee, of the Fourth Iowa Cavalry, had succeeded, with a detachment of that regiment, in gaining a position on the same side with the Rebels and the brigade of General Brown had been ordered to the front. As soon as the command devolved upon me I dismounted the Third Iowa Cavalry, Maj. B.S. Jones commanding, and advanced them as skirmishers toward the enemy, through the woods that lined the immediate banks of the creek, until I arrived at an open space, some 200 yards in width, on the near side of which I found 200 or 300 men of the Missouri State Militia posted behind some houses at which the enemy was pouring a very hot fire. By dint of great urging and exertion of authority, I succeeded in getting them from behind their places of shelter, and then, with them and my dismounted men, advanced across the field at a double-quick to the woods beyond; the enemy at the same time resisting us stoutly. The woods attained, we pushed the enemy rapidly through them to the prairie beyond, where he had stationed a battery, from which he played among us shell after shell. My command, nevertheless moved on and with such great rapidity that the Rebel commander, fearing, I suppose, for the safety of his cannon, withdrew them with his command rapidly and fell back quite a distance across the prairie beyond even the range of artillery. In the meantime I had sent for the Fourth Iowa Cavalry and dismounted them and advanced them in line of skirmishers as a support to my advanced line. The enemy thus for the moment having been pushed beyond our reach, my whole command was brought forward on the prairie, and after a few minutes being allowed to rest the whole was mounted, and, at your direction, I moved out on what was called the ridge road toward the position the enemy had taken. It had now got to be past noon, and after some distance had been gained, I sent Captain Young to find you and obtain the permission to feed our hungry animals. The captain shortly after reporting that he could not ascertain your whereabouts, I took the responsibility to halt my command in a large cornfield and take a few minutes to feed. I had not taken too much time when I perceived that there was work to be done, as I could plainly see a battle raging in our front, and immediately ordered my men into the saddle and moved out on a trot toward the State line. A few minutes sufficed to bring us to the scene of the conflict. Here I found the enemy making a charge and some of our troops falling ingloriously back. I tried, with the assistance of

Captain Young, to rally them, but without avail. I then ordered my leading regiment, the Tenth Missouri Cavalry, to form a line to the left and ordered them to make a counter charge, which they did in gallant style, turning the Rebels and driving them. I then formed the rest of my brigade and ordered a charge, in which the whole command participated, driving the enemy far beyond the battle-ground, beyond Missouri into Kansas and beyond the town of Santa Fe. In this charge Second Lieut. M.C. Auld, Company I, Tenth Missouri Cavalry was severely wounded. Our horses having become jaded and worn down, I formed my column and proceeded to a point just beyond the Kansas line and about two miles and a half from Santa Fe, and halted to rest both animals and men. Here I received orders from you to go into camp for the night and in the morning move out and meet you at or near the last named town.

On the morning of the 24th, just after daylight, we moved out to Santa Fe, and taking our position just in the rear of General Sanborn's command marched until late that night, reaching the Osage River, where, on the order of General Sanborn, we bivouacked around the home of Elder Williams, that officer deeming it too dark and the enemy too well posted for an attack that night. That day we marched over desolated country where even water was scarce, at a speed that necessarily kept the rear at a trot, and bivouacked, without forage for our jaded horses, a distance of at least forty-two miles. The morning of the 25th broke and gave promise of a dull and dreary day, when I was ordered with my brigade to march to the river and cross, receiving from you the order to charge the enemy whenever the opportunity offered. I crossed, and reaching the prairie formed my column in the following order: First, the Tenth Missouri Cavalry, Maj. W.H. Lusk; second, the Fourth Iowa Cavalry, Maj. A.R. Pierce; third, the Third Iowa Cavalry, Maj. B.S. Jones, and fourth, the Seventh Indiana Cavalry and Fourth Missouri Cavalry, consolidated, under the command of Major S.E.W. Simonson, of the former regiment, and moved as rapidly as possible after the retreating enemy. The skies now cleared, and the sun smiled out upon the scene as if foretelling the glorious day that awaited us. After forming, a few advanced skirmishers were thrown out to prevent a too sudden approach upon the enemy, who might be behind any of the numerous hills of the undulating prairie. Three short miles were scarcely accomplished when one of the advanced skirmishers galloped back and reported that the enemy was only a few hundred yards away in line of battle, in large force, and with eight pieces of artillery. About the same time Major Hunt, of General Curtis' staff, came up and told me the enemy's exact position, stating that there was a brigade already in positions in his front, but too weak to begin the attack. I at once determined to form on the left of this brigade, especially as a few more paces brought us in view of the Rebels; seeing the position in which he had his artillery, I immediately surmised that the Rebel commander had committed a fatal blunder, and resolved to capture it. I sent an officer to the commanding officer of the brigade on my right with the information that I was going to charge, and a request for him to charge with me, for god's sake, and at the same time formed my command in column of regiments in the same manner I had formed them for marching, and immediately sounded the charge. The line of the brigade on my right was soon passed, but it did not charge with us; this brigade I have since learned was the one commanded by Col. J.F. Phillips of the Missouri State Militia. The fire of the enemy was now so hot that for a moment it staggered even my own gallant regiment, but it soon recovered and went on with an exulting yell. At the time the charge was sounded, I gave the orders for the different regiments to execute a right half-wheel, and dispatched my staff to see it executed, then to completely cut off the enemy's chance to escape with his artillery. This maneuver was successfully executed, and we captured the guns in a shorted space of time than is necessary to record it. Then began a fierce hand-to-hand fight, one that surpassed for the time it lasted than I have ever witnessed.

My loss in this part of the day's transaction was large, but in comparison with the gains it was small. Lieutenant Curtiss, of the Fourth Iowa was instantly killed while gallantly encouraging on his men, and Lieut. B. Armbrust, Company A, Fourth Cavalry Missouri Volunteers, was wounded in the bridle arm while bravely charging at the head of his company. The enemy was completely routed and driven in the wildest confusion from the field; several of his wagons were abandoned in the narrow road that crosses the creek just in the rear of his position. Many of his force lay dead and wounded upon the field and in our hands. It is a matter of impossibility for me to state the number, as I had no opportunity of passing over the scene of the conflict afterward. After the action of the morning my brigade took no part in any fighting, until the final one of the day, when the enemy drew up his whole force on the afternoon upon what I am informed is called the Little Marmiton Creek. In this action I formed my command as you ordered for a charge as follows: The Tenth Missouri line of battle, the Third and Fourth Iowa, and Major Simonson's command in column of squadrons in their rear, and with the intention to charge as soon as a striking distance could be reached. I ordered the charge at one time, but the enemy fell back too rapidly upon his strong lines and I felt that it would be more than useless to continue, so I halted and formed a line of battle, my ammunition by this time being reduced to a very few rounds per man and my horses being completely tired out. Major Stinson's command was not included in the line of battle, as you had stationed him to support the section of artillery you had stationed to the left and rear of the command.

In this last action we lost several men wounded, and amongst them was Maj. A.R. Pierce, of the Fourth Iowa Cavalry, who was severely wounded in the foot while leading his men toward the Rebels. He did not leave the field until the night set in and the command bivouacked on the field, the enemy meantime having retired. This ended the fighting up to the present time in which we have had any participation. The next morning I moved my command to Fort Scott halting to feed on the road. The next day I received orders from you to report to Major-General Curtis, and am at present still under his orders.

This report does not pretend to give any history of our operations previous to my assumption of command. I suppose Colonel Winslow, my predecessor, will make his report as soon as possible of the movements up to the time of his departure.

*You will find annexed Exhibit A, * which gives a list of the casualties of the command for the whole period of time the command has been in pursuit of Price. Hundreds of prisoners have fallen into our hands, but owing to the nature of our movements, I have not been able to keep a record of them.*

My thanks are due to the officers and men for their gallant and cheerful performance of duty at all times. Maj. W.H. Lush, of the Tenth Missouri; Maj. A.R. Pierce, of the Fourth Iowa; Maj. B.S. Jones, of the Third Iowa; Maj. S.E.W. Simonson, of the Seventh Indiana, and Captain Knipsel, of the Fourth Missouri, are entitled to especial mention for the brave examples they set their men and the gallant style in which they led them into danger. To Private James Dunlavy, Company D, Third Iowa Cavalry, belongs the honor of capturing Major General Marmaduke, and to Sergt. Calvary M. Young, of the same company [Company L] *and regiment, that of taking General Cabell. We also captured besides the guns and prisoners two stand of colors. Of my staff, I beg particularly to mention Capt. J.F. Young, Tenth Missouri Cavalry, acting assistant adjutant-general, and Lieut. August Thiel, of the Fourth Missouri Cavalry, acting aide-de-camp for their gallantry in the field and their unceasing attention to duty at all times. I did not desire to make any invidious distinctions, however, for all did well and nobly and deserve the thanks of their country.*

> *In conclusion, allow me, general, to return you my sincerest thanks for the uniform kindness you have displayed toward me during our official connection, and I shall always cherish it with the kindest of feelings and regard.*
>
> *I remain, very respectfully, your obedient servant,*
> *F.W. Benteen, Lieut. Col. Tenth Cavalry Missouri Vols., Comdg. Fourth Brig.*
> *Maj. Gen. A. Pleasonton.*

Clearly, this after-action report gives a sense of being on the battlefield with Benteen and his cavalry troopers. The vivid nature with which he conveyed the action that his brigade undertook is spelled out more clearly than any historian can do. Benteen and his men were pivotal to the actions on October 25, 1864, and will be remembered for years to come. The gallantry that he and his men showed on the field of battle helped to send Price and his army ingloriously back to Rebel territory and signaled the end of Confederate aggression in the Trans-Mississippi theater of the Civil War.

Bibliography

Bevier, R.S. *History of the First and Second Missouri Confederate Brigades 1861–1865 and from Wakarusa to Appomattox: A Military Anagraph.* St. Louis, MO: Bryan, Brand & Company, 1879.

Buresh, Lumir. *October 25th and the Battle of Mine Creek.* Kansas City, MO: Lowell Press, 1977.

Castel, Albert. *Civil War Kansas: Reaping the Whirlwind.* Lawrence: University of Kansas Press, 1958.

———. *A Frontier State at War: Kansas 1861–1865.* Lawrence, KS: Kansas Heritage Press, 1958.

Cates, Stephen B. *Confederate Cavalry West of the River.* Austin: University of Texas Press, 1961.

Davis, George B., Major, United States Army, Leslie J. Perry and Mr. Joseph W. Kirkley, Board of Publication. *The War of the Rebellion: Official Records of the Union and Confederate Armies.* Series I, Vol. 41, *Price's Missouri Expedition, Etc.* Washington, D.C.: Government Printing Office, 1893.

Du Bois, W.E.B., and John David Smith. *John Brown: A Biography.* Armonk, NY: M.E. Sharpe, Inc., 1997.

Edwards, John N. *Edwards, Shelby and His Men or The War in the West.* Cincinnati, OH: Miami Printing & Publishing Company, 1867.

Etcheson, Nicole. *Bleeding Kansas: Contested Liberty in the Civil War Era.* Lawrence: University of Kansas Press, 2004.

Gott, Kendall D., Senior Historian, U.S. Army Combat Studies Institute. Interview with the author. Fort Leavenworth, Kansas.

Harrold, Stanley. *Border War: Fighting Over Slavery Before the Civil War.* Chapel Hill: University of North Carolina Press, 2010.

Josephy, Alvin, Jr. *The Civil War in the American West.* New York: Alfred A. Knopf, 1991.

Matlin, James C. *Judge Lecompte and the "Sack of Lawrence" May 21st 1856.* Topeka: Kansas Historical Quarterly, Kansas State Historical Society, 1953.

Monaghan, Jay. *Civil War on the Western Border, 1864–65.* New York: Bonanza Books, 1955.

Neely, Jeremy. *The Border Between Them: Violence and Reconciliation of the Kansas—Missouri Line.* Columbia: University of Missouri Press, 2007.

Orman, Ray P. *The Repeal of the Missouri Compromise: Its Origin and Authorship.* Boston, MA: J.S. Canner & Company Inc., 1965.

Phillips, Christopher. *Missouri's Confederate: Claiborne Fox Jackson and the Creation of Southern Identity in the Border West.* Columbia: University of Missouri Press, 2000.

Reynolds, David S. *John Brown, Abolitionist: The Man Who Killed Slavery, Sparked the Civil War, and Seeded Civil Rights.* New York: Vintage, 2006.

Scott, William Forse. *The Story of a Cavalry Regiment.* New York: G.P. Putnam's Sons, 1893.

Starr, Stephen Z. *Jennison's Jayhawkers: A Civil War Cavalry Regiment and Its Commander.* Baton Rouge: Louisiana State University Press, 1973.

———. *The Union Cavalry in the Civil War.* Vol. 8, *The War in the West.* Baton Rouge: Louisiana State University Press, 1985.

Wunder, John R., and Joan M. Rodd, eds. *The Nebraska-Kansas Act of 1854.* Lincoln: University of Nebraska Press, 2008.

Index

M

N

O

P

Q

R

S

About the Author

Jeff Stalnaker lives in Mission, Kansas, with his wife, Jen, his daughter, Emma, and two dogs and a cat. He has a degree from the University of Kansas, with an emphasis in history and political science, is an avid student of history and is a local Kansas City singer/songwriter. He is also a World War II living historian, reenacting both the U.S. Army and British army.